The Awe of God

The
Awe
of
God

The Astounding Way a Healthy Fear of God Transforms Your Life

JOHN BEVERE

W PUBLISHING GROUP

AN IMPRINT OF THOMAS NELSON

*My magnificent wife, best friend, and
cherished love, Lisa Bevere.*

"A woman who fears the LORD will be greatly praised."
PROVERBS 31:30

*I wrote this book in our fortieth year of marriage.
Each year with you only gets better, and if given the
chance, I would marry you again in a heartbeat.
No words can express the delight and
joy you bring to my heart.
I would not be the man I am today had it
not been for your love and support.
You are wise, fun, delightful, strong,
adventurous, and gorgeous.
I love you forever.*

CONTENTS

Contents

WEEK 4: OUR RESPONSE TO GOD'S WORD

WEEK 5: INTIMACY WITH GOD

WEEK 6: THE TREASURE'S BENEFITS

HOW TO JOURNEY THROUGH THIS BOOK

Dear Reader,

This isn't just any message; it's a life message that, if believed and acted on, will transform you forever. I am confident in this because these truths have changed my life and countless others'. Whenever I'm asked for advice—whether it's about marriage, family, or ministry—my immediate go-to is what's contained in this book.

Due to its importance, a lot of time and contemplative prayers have gone into how to present it. Considering the ebb and flow of our lives today—the demands of our schedules and the rapid pace at which we move—I felt the need to adapt and present the truths in bite-sized chunks so that you will be able to deeply ponder these small bits.

At first glance you may think this is a devotional, but I assure you it's not. Let me explain. A devotional often has different topics for each day that don't necessarily build into a concise and systematic message. Even though this book may look like a devotional, each day builds on the previous day's chapter to form what is typically found in a full nonfiction book. The advantage of this is that you can decide how to read it. It certainly can be read in a day or two, if that is your preference; however, I strongly recommend you read it in either a six-week period (a chapter a day) or a three-week period (a chapter in the morning and another in the evening).

At the conclusion of each chapter, you will find five tools to help deepen the benefit of its content—we'll call this section "Making it Personal," and it contains the 5 Ps:

1. **Passage:** I will include a passage from Scripture that is crucial to that day's message found in the body of the text, or one that was not brought up in the main body of that chapter but adds strength to what was presented. I highly recommend memorizing these passages.

2. **Point:** This is a main thought contained within the chapter to drive home its importance. Seeing it again will strengthen its effectiveness and give you a quick reference when coming back and reviewing the chapter.

3. **Ponder:** This is crucial. The psalmist states, "I will meditate on Your precepts, and contemplate Your ways" (Psalm 119:15 NKJV). We meditate by rolling over in our minds how the Word of God applies to us in our present state. In doing so we are told our ways will be prosperous and we will have good success (see Joshua 1:8, Psalm 1, and 1 Timothy 4:15).

4. **Prayer:** There will also be a prayer that reflects the teaching of the chapter. It's so important that God hears our voice and that we give Him the permission to change us according to His Word.

5. **Profession:** We are told that *death and life* are in the power of what we say (see Proverbs 18:21). In speaking what He declares over us, our spirit, soul, and body come into alignment with His will for us, which is the proven way to experience life to the fullest.

Again, I encourage you to take your time going through this book so the truths from God's Word penetrate your heart and mind. Spending the coming weeks dwelling on these truths daily will help them to sink in and take root in your life. This is more than mere information; it is the path to growing closer to our God. I also recommend that you read the chapters and go through each of the 5 Ps in "Making It Personal" with a journal alongside you. Put your thoughts and prayers into the journal each day so that when you return to it later you can refer to what the Holy Spirit revealed to your mind.

A few more recommendations: First, with your smartphone or watch, time how long it takes you to read a chapter, go through "Making It Personal," and journal. Don't rush; it's not a race. The reason for the timer is so that after several chapters you will be able to wisely plan for the future chapters based on your average time.

Second, try to develop a habit, and don't allow anything to interfere with your set time each day. It's my prayer and hope that what God has done in me over the past forty years He will do with you as you go through this book.

Third, a message always brings the greatest benefit when I teach it or go through it with a group of friends. Choose some close friends and work through this together. After you complete the chapter on your own, with just you and the Holy Spirit, get together with your friends to share what He showed you. Do this on a regular basis.

If you'd like a group format, we've also developed an *Awe of God* Bible study with video curriculum and study guide that you and your friends can go through together on a weekly basis.[1] It offers even more tools to discuss the Word of God. Scripture says, "Then those who feared the LORD spoke with each other, and the LORD listened to what they said. In his presence, a scroll of remembrance was written to record the names of those who feared him and always thought about the honor of his name" (Malachi 3:16).

Finally, we have 42 short videos that highlight the core truths from each chapter. To access them, go to Appendix A and scan the QR code. There you'll also find information on video curriculum for small group study and other bonus content.

I pray you grow more intimate with God as you journey through *Awe of God*. It's important to read the introduction rather than skipping to chapter 1, as it opens our hearts to what we will be discussing. And when you've finished the book, I'd love to hear from you how your faith and life have been impacted through a holy fear of God.

Sincerely,
John Bevere

P.S. Just a reminder to not skip the introduction. It is my prayer that it will ignite a fire in you to cultivate a holy awe and dive headfirst into this message.

INTRODUCTION

Fear. For years people have strived to eradicate it. Many have researched it, fought it, and campaigned to remove its influence from our lives. Even the famous quote by President Franklin D. Roosevelt calls attention to it: "The only thing we have to fear is fear itself." Voices across all platforms shout that we need to find ways to overcome fear, and we can find hundreds if not thousands of self-help books designed to do exactly that. Since the late 1980s people everywhere have worn clothing with the words "No Fear" printed boldly across it. We seem adamant in our quest to eliminate all fear from our lives.

This crusade seems sensible, noble, and prudent; and while on many fronts it is, the truth is, *not all fear is bad*. So why the obsession? I believe it stems from lumping all fears into one big category under the label of "harmful." But is this assumption accurate?

First, it is important to acknowledge that there are indeed *destructive* fears, even when they seem sensible. If we fear losing all our money and possessions, we will likely obsess over them and become misers and hoarders, worshiping our money and assets over everything else. If we fear losing a spouse, we will cling to that person too tightly or be suspicious of their every action. Either way, it leads to resentment and eventually damages the relationship. If we have a deep fear of missing out—FOMO—it might cause us to chase new excitements and new experiences, but it will be at the expense of healthy community, real connection, and the beautiful peace that accompanies commitment. If we fear for the safety of our kids, we will likely thwart their growth by smothering them or by fostering prodigal behavior. The list is seemingly endless.

On the other hand, *constructive* fears produce beneficial wisdom. The fear of falling two thousand feet off a cliff gives us the wisdom not to step too close to the edge, where we might slip. The fear of a grizzly bear's power gives us the wisdom not to threaten the mother bear's cubs. The fear of a third-degree burn gives us the wisdom to put protective mitts on our hands when removing a pan from a hot oven.

And yet, constructive fear, although beneficial, can also be perverted and diminish our lives. Left unchecked, the fear of falling can keep us from getting on a plane, thus grounding us. The unrestrained terror of that grizzly bear can deprive us of a pleasant walk in the woods, and the fear of burning ourselves could keep us from turning on the oven and enjoying a home-cooked meal.

The real question we should be asking is, *What do we fear most?* This is a much better inquiry than focusing on how to annihilate destructive fears or manage constructive ones. It's a wise question, and if properly answered, it puts all other fears into perspective and enhances our lives—both now and eternally. It illuminates the path to a good and fulfilling life. The Bible has much to say about fear, and the building block is this: the fear of the Lord is the beginning of wisdom (Proverbs 1:7), and not just any wisdom, but God's wisdom. That's not a bad place to start.

So consider this: What if fear—rightly aimed—is a *virtue*? What if the fear of God is the paradoxical path to an authentic relationship with Him? And what if this holy fear is what truly opens us up to the fullness of life that Jesus followers have experienced throughout the centuries? What if this fear eradicates all other fears—the fear of starting your own business, the fear of what your government will do, the fear of what will happen to your children, the fear a hypochondriac suffers from, the fear that causes mental illness or depression (a list that could continue endlessly)?

As we begin our journey, please allow me to make four statements of truth:

1. We are human, and we will fear.
2. The awe and fear of God is way deeper, more beautiful, and more intimate than many dare imagine.
3. The fear of God swallows up all destructive fears.
4. The fear of God is the beginning of everything good.

Some folks will rightly remind us that the Bible tells us—about 365 times—to "fear not," and this leads many Christians to conclude that God does not want us to fear. But these verses refer to *destructive* fear. Additionally, I can point out almost 200 verses in the Bible that encourage us to "fear God." And here's the unfortunate part: in our quest to try to eliminate any fear in our lives (including the virtue of fearing God), this area of our faith has been left unexamined, untried, and without benefit.

The fear of the Lord is more glorious, more awe-inspiring, and even more joyous than we could ever imagine. As we continue, I want to show you how rightly directed fear—specifically the virtue of fearing God above all else—opens up the path to a life beyond what you have ever imagined. And it's only then that we are able to boldly address anything that life may throw at us. In the words of Charles Spurgeon, "The fear of God is the death of every other fear; like a mighty lion, it chases all other fears before it."[1]

My hope as you read this book is that you will dive headfirst into this virtue, peel away the religious façade of what it is not, and uncover the goodness of how it sets our feet on solid ground. Yes, fear no evil—but discover how the misunderstood virtue of fearing the Lord will cause your life to blossom into something wildly beautiful.

Let's start with an exploration of how awesome our God is.

We'll call it the "Awe of God"!

An Awesome God

Fear of the Lord is His treasure, a choice jewel, given only to . . . those who are greatly beloved.

—JOHN BUNYAN

1 | GOD'S TREASURE

What if you were told of a hidden virtue that in essence is the key to all of life? It unlocks the purpose of your existence and attracts the presence, protection, and providence of your Creator. It is the root of all noble character, the foundation of all happiness, and provides needed adjustments to all inharmonious circumstances you may face. Firmly embracing this virtue could lengthen your life, procure good health, ensure success and safety, eliminate lack, and guarantee a noble legacy.

Sound too good to be true? You might be wondering, *Is this book I hold fiction?* I assure you it's not—what I've stated is truth.

If presented with this reality, most might sneer and retort, "No such virtue exists!" Yet every promise above was written by undoubtably one of the wisest men to ever live, and even more, he wrote these words under the inspiration of our Creator—and His words are infallible!

However, prior to Solomon's departure from this life, he fell from the bliss he scribed because his heart deserted the Source of his wisdom and he consequently strayed from the path of living well.

Allow me to give a brief account of his story. As a child Solomon was trained in and embraced this virtue. He grew strong in noble character and developed keen insight. He excelled quickly in leadership and eventually became ruler over millions. After his request to God, he possessed astounding wisdom; in fact, very little was difficult for him to understand. He wrote thousands of wise sayings and composed hundreds of songs: "He could speak with authority about all kinds of plants, from the great cedar of Lebanon to the tiny hyssop that grows from cracks in a wall. He could also speak about animals, birds, small creatures, and fish" (1 Kings 4:33).

This wise man achieved a level of success, fortune, and fame that was unmatched before and has not been experienced since. Kings, queens, ambassadors, and high-level leaders would travel great distances to be in his presence, hear his insights, witness the excellence and unity of his team, and be impacted by the innovation that produced his nation's great strength and wealth. He was so impressive that one queen didn't believe the reports she heard prior to her visit. However, after spending time with him, she exclaimed, "'I had not heard the half of it! Your wisdom and prosperity are far beyond what I was told. How happy your people must be! What a privilege for your officials to stand here day after day, listening to your wisdom!'" (1 Kings 10:7–8).

From what we read, the people he led were happy and effective in their endeavors. Poverty was nonexistent; every family in his kingdom owned their own house and garden. History reports the people "were very contented, with plenty to eat and drink" (1 Kings 4:20). They lived in peace and safety.

As time passed, however, this notable leader eventually stepped away from what fueled his achievements. He became wise in his own eyes and deemed it no longer necessary to heed the wisdom of this virtue. He lost his way and eventually became a bitter cynic. He was not the only one to suffer from his misjudgment—so, too, did those he led.

To him, life became meaningless. He wrote disparaging statements such as, "Everything's boring, utterly boring—no one can find any meaning in it,"[1] and "History merely repeats itself as there is nothing new under the sun."[2] Even more dramatic, he stated, "The day you die is better than the day

4

you're born,"[3] and "What is wrong cannot be made right. What is missing cannot be recovered."[4] In fact, he wrote an entire book depicting the scope of life's pointless existence; to him, all was vanity. This one man, in a relatively short time, plummeted from the highest heights of success to the deepest recesses of a flagrant pessimism. Many psychologists today would diagnosis him as suffering from a severe case of manic depression. How could one man span such extremes?

The good news: His story doesn't end in the depths of despondency. He eventually returned to life's most important virtue. We don't know how many months or even years he spent writing his dismal book, but his final chapter gives a glimpse into his recovery. He begins by writing seven[5] times in one form or another, "Remember your Creator," with his final words being:

> All has been heard; the end of the matter is: *Fear God* . . . and keep His commandments, for this is the whole of man [the full, original purpose of his creation, the object of God's providence, the root of character, the foundation of all happiness, the adjustment to all inharmonious circumstances and conditions under the sun] *and* the whole [duty] for every man. (Ecclesiastes 12:13 AMPC)

The prized virtue is none other than *the fear of God*. The writer, King Solomon, declares it as the prerequisite to a fulfilling, abundant life. We read in Scripture, "Who are those who *fear* the LORD? He will show them the *path* they should choose" (Psalm 25:12). This path is uncommon because, sadly, many believe, as King Solomon did in his dark hours, that their own wisdom is what brings success and happiness. Holy fear keeps us connected to the wisdom of our Creator—the only One who knows what enhances us and what undoes us.

Holy fear's importance so vastly trumps all other virtues that Scripture identifies it as Jesus' *delight* (Isaiah 11:3 NKJV), and just as incredible, "The fear of the LORD is His [God's] *treasure*" (Isaiah 33:6 NKJV). Stop and ponder this for a moment: it's God Almighty's *delight* and *treasure*. Astounding!

We'll dive deeper into this amazing reality shortly, but first back to King Solomon.

Why would I open this message with his success, failure, and ultimate recovery? In my first few years of ministry, a wise leader made an attention-grabbing statement that's stayed with me for decades. He declared, "I've made it a general principle to refrain from promoting anyone to a place of authority whose record is perfect."

When asked why, he answered, "I learn more about a person's character by their response to failure than anything else. Did they own responsibility, repent, and grow from the experience? Or did they justify their behavior and delegate the blame? It shows if he or she is fit for responsibility." What I learned from that was: *it indicates if wisdom is what he or she prizes above all else.*

Solomon didn't fully realize the value of godly fear, even though he taught it under the inspiration of the Holy Spirit! Therefore, it was possible for him to be drawn away from it. Prior to his fall, godly fear wasn't his *treasure* or *delight*; it wasn't an immovable foundation for his motives and actions. In stumbling, experiencing folly, and finally recovering, he more fully grasped the magnitude of its power.

In a similar light, the apostle Paul wrote:

> I buffet my body . . . and subdue it, for *fear* that after proclaiming to others the Gospel and things pertaining to it, I myself should become unfit [not stand the test, be unapproved and rejected as a counterfeit]. (1 Corinthians 9:27 AMPC)

Paul understood the importance of treasuring the wisdom entrusted to him by God's Spirit and of not making the same tragic error as King Solomon. The hidden truths of God's covenant were revealed to him, which would free multitudes, but if he didn't see godly *fear* as invaluable and firmly embrace it, he too would also end up a hopeless cynic—unfit, unapproved, and rejected as a counterfeit.

Embracing godly fear as our most prized treasure empowers us to remain under submission to truth, and in so doing, it keeps us on the path of life, which brings remarkable rewards.

In a time when most regard fear as detrimental or damaging, to declare the *fear of the Lord* as a beneficial and prized virtue seems counterintuitive. However, based on the authority of Scripture, I assure you that when we embrace it, we will be empowered to remain on the path of life. Here we will experience true intimacy with God and life-altering benefits—one of the greatest of which is being transformed into the image of Jesus Christ. So let's commence our journey of discovering the awe of God.

Making It Personal

Passage: And there shall be stability in your times, an abundance of salvation, wisdom, and knowledge; the reverent fear and worship of the Lord is your treasure and His. (Isaiah 33:6 AMPC)

Point: Holy fear is God's treasure; it should be ours.

Ponder: What does it look like, practically, to treasure holy fear? How should I approach it? How should I handle it? How do I not lose it?

Prayer: Dear heavenly Father, I ask that on this journey of discovering the fear of the Lord, I will come to know it, live by it, and delight in it. May it become my treasure, as it is Yours. May it give me the wisdom and knowledge needed to live a fulfilled and successful life, one that is pleasing in Your sight. Also, may those who are dear to me be enlightened, and may all who interact with me recognize its value. I ask this in the name of Jesus Christ, my Lord and Savior, amen.

Profession: I choose to value holy fear as life's great treasure, and in doing so I will be strengthened to remain on the path of living well.

Fear God, yes, but don't be afraid of Him.

—J. A. SPENDER

2 | CONTRASTING FEARS

In the summer of 1994, I was asked to minister for a church conference in the Southeastern United States. It was a large congregation that two years earlier had experienced a powerful four-week awakening led by a world-famous evangelist. The revival emphasized God's goodness, love, and joy; it affected many lives in a beautiful way. But sadly, the church remained fixated on the experience of the revival and didn't continue to further know the heart of God. In essence, they'd become stuck and out of balance.

At the time, I was on a journey to discover holy fear. I could see its importance but was still growing in my knowledge of it and was therefore hesitant to share on it publicly. Even so, I strongly sensed the need to lay aside this apprehension and minister on the fear of the Lord in the first evening session.

I took the platform and began to speak from my limited understanding to the congregation. It didn't help my confidence that the people stared at me with blank looks on their faces, completely unresponsive. It seemed my words were falling on deaf ears. As it happened, I was correct, and I would learn why soon enough.

The next evening after worship the head pastor took the platform for what I assumed would be a routine introduction, but this wasn't the case. For fifteen minutes he corrected what I had spoken about the previous evening. He confidently stated, "The fear of the Lord only applies to Old Testament times, but as Christians, we've not been given 'a spirit of fear,'" referencing 2 Timothy 1:7.

I sat in the front row utterly shocked and felt I was in the middle of a nightmare. The longer he spoke, the more uncomfortable it became. He continued, "We are told in the New Testament, 'There is no fear in love; but perfect love casts out fear' [1 John 4:18 NKJV]. So, what John taught last evening is error, and I want to protect you from it." His elaborate correction of my message continued for several more minutes.

Once he finished, to my surprise, he introduced me to the platform to minister. I still remember walking up and thinking to myself, *How can I minister to these people after what he just did? This can't be happening.* But it was happening, and I had to pull myself together when all I wanted to do was run. It was difficult to keep a thought, let alone speak a life-giving message to the people attending the conference.

As I spoke, my mind kept reverting back to his correction; I couldn't shake his words. The experience felt both surreal and horrific. I had to harness my thoughts several times while speaking to stay on track. I fought off feelings telling me, *Forget this, stop speaking, and get out of here.* It was miserable. After a short message, I turned the service over to him, returned quickly to the hotel, and went to bed utterly bewildered and feeling like an outcast.

The next morning, I found a quiet construction site near my hotel; there were no workers on the jobsite. I prayed earnestly, anticipating God's correction. With sincerity, I asked, "Lord, have I hurt Your church? Have I taught something untrue? Am I putting Your people in bondage?"

I continued for quite some time, and as I prayed, what I uttered began to change. I stopped doubting my message from that evening and found myself passionately asking for more understanding of holy fear. It was a plea coming from deep in my heart, and I was surprised by what was happening. I didn't sense God's dissatisfaction but rather His pleasure in what I had done. He began to bring to my remembrance numerous scriptures in the New Testament regarding the fear of the Lord. In time I found myself no longer befuddled but now crying out in a loud, passionate voice, "Father, I want to know the fear of the Lord, I want to walk in it!"

The New Testament writers did write the words the pastor quoted, but they also penned other statements:

- The apostle Paul writes, "Work out your own salvation with *fear* and *trembling*" (Philippians 2:12 NKJV).
- Again, he instructs, "Beloved, let us cleanse ourselves from all filthiness of the flesh and spirit, perfecting holiness in *the fear of God*" (2 Corinthians 7:1 NKJV).
- The writer of Hebrews pens, "Let us have grace, by which we may serve God acceptably with *reverence* and *godly fear*" (Hebrews 12:28 NKJV).
- The apostle Peter writes, "If you call on the Father, who without partiality judges according to each one's work, conduct yourselves throughout the time of your stay here *in fear*" (1 Peter 1:17 NKJV).
- The apostle Jude declares, "Save with *fear*" (Jude v. 23 NKJV).
- And Jesus urges us, "And do not fear those who kill the body but cannot kill the soul. But rather fear Him who is able to destroy both soul and body in hell" (Matthew 10:28 NKJV).

I could continue, and certainly will as we progress, but I hope you get the point: *Holy fear* is a New Testament truth. These are but a few of the scriptures the Lord brought to my heart as I prayed.

I realized that morning the pastor had confused the "spirit of fear" with the "fear of the Lord." There is a huge difference, and it is illustrated by what took place when Moses led the nation of Israel to Mount Sinai to meet with God.

Once the entire nation arrives, Moses goes up for an initial private meeting. The Almighty reveals the purpose behind His powerful deliverance:

> Thus you shall say to the house of Jacob, and tell the children of Israel: "You have seen what I did to the Egyptians, and how I bore you on eagles' wings and *brought you to Myself.*" (Exodus 19:3–4 NKJV)

The chief reason for God's mighty deliverance was to gather *all the people* to Himself. He longed for them and desired a meeting so they could know Him as Moses did. However, three days later, when God comes down on the mountain to introduce Himself, the people respond by quickly retreating. In terror they cry out to Moses, "'You speak with us, and we will hear; but let not God speak with us, lest we die'" (Exodus 20:19 NKJV). In an attempt to console them, their leader replies, "'*Do not fear*; for God has come to test you, and that *His fear may be before you,* so that you may not sin'" (Exodus 20:20 NKJV).

At first glance it seems Moses contradicts himself: "Do not fear" because God has come "that His fear may be before you." Is he speaking out of both sides of his mouth? The answer is no. Moses is merely differentiating between being "scared of God" and having "the fear of the Lord." Again, there is a huge difference.

Someone who's scared of God has something to hide. Recall, in the garden, once Adam sinned, he and Eve hid from the presence of the Lord. Their reaction wasn't unique to them; similar behavioral responses exist throughout Scripture in those who venture into darkness.

However, the person who fears God has nothing to hide. He or she is terrified of being away from God. This is illustrated by the fact that while the people drew back, Moses simultaneously drew nearer to God. The person who fears God doesn't say within themselves, "How close can I get to the line of sin and not fall in?" No, he or she says, "I want to be so close to God, and so far away from that line, that I can't even see it."

So, before defining what holy fear is and discussing its benefits, let's first clarify what it is not. *It is not being scared of God and therefore withdrawing from Him.* How can we enjoy intimacy with someone we're afraid of? Pulling away is the opposite of what He desires. In Psalms we read, "My heart has heard you say, 'Come and talk with me.' And my heart responds,

'LORD, I am coming'" (Psalm 27:8). Do you hear the call to intimacy? He desires for you to come close, to interact, laugh together, share together, and do life together. The psalmist also writes, "The LORD is a friend to those who fear him" (25:14). The firm reality is this: God wants to be close and intimate with you. So rest assured, holy fear does not quench intimacy; it does just the opposite—it enhances our interaction with God.

Making It Personal

Passage: "Don't be afraid. God has come to test you and instill a deep and reverent awe within you so that you won't sin." (Exodus 20:20 MSG)

Point: Holy fear is not to be scared of God and thereby withdraw from Him. It is to be terrified of being away from Him.

Ponder: What was the main purpose for God delivering Israel out of Egypt? What is the main purpose for God delivering me from slavery to the bondages of the world?

Prayer: Dear heavenly Father, thank You for delivering me from a spirit of fear through my Lord Jesus Christ. I ask You to instill in me holy fear that I may not sin against You, for this would take away from the intimacy You desire with me and I desire with You. I ask this in Jesus' name, amen.

Profession: God has called me to be intimate with Him; therefore, I'm not scared of God, but I do desire to fear Him so that I may not sin.

To fear God, is one of the first and greatest Duties of his rational Creatures.

—CHARLES INGLIS

3 | WHAT IS HOLY FEAR?

It's impossible to define holy fear in a single sentence, paragraph, or chapter. It's no different from attempting to explain the full breadth of God's love in the same space. It will take chapters, and even then, we'll be far from proficient in our understanding. In fact, I believe we'll continue to discover the depths of both holy love and holy fear throughout eternity.

With that said, let me offer a general outline of holy fear's definition. Think back to your childhood when you were given a coloring book and crayons. You opened the book, picked out a page, and found an outline waiting to be filled in with color. In a similar way, this chapter will give us the borders, but it will take the rest of the book to fill in the colors. If you were to read only this chapter, you'd get a broad idea of holy fear but would miss out on its transformational truths.

In the previous chapter we established that the fear of the Lord doesn't drive us from God's presence—rather just the opposite. A good and wonderful fear draws us close to Him, and laying this firm foundation is vital before we continue.

Some say that the fear of the Lord only means to reverently worship God. I've heard these very words spoken by well-known ministers from the pulpit, in conversations, and over a meal with leaders. While this definition is a start, it's far from the complete picture. It could be compared to merely defining the love of God as being "patient and kind" (1 Corinthians 13:4). But if we leave it there, we fall short and miss the mark completely.

When Lisa and I were in our early forties, the son-in-law of a well-respected leader visited our house to share an opportunity to invest in his company. We met for a couple of hours, and I distinctly remember the kindness and patience he showed us. If you observed his behavior, you too would affirm he's a loving man. However, after several days of prayer, Lisa and I didn't feel led to invest. Now, years later, I'm glad we didn't, because he spent many years in the penitentiary for running a massive Ponzi scheme.

Was the man patient and kind? Most definitely. Did he walk in love? Absolutely not. Why? Because Scripture tells us, "This is the love of God, that we keep His commandments" (1 John 5:3 NKJV). Stealing is selfish and breaks God's commandment of love (Ephesians 4:28). A child molester can be kind, and even patient, while at the same time destroying a young person's life. Does he love that child? Of course not!

In the same way, limiting holy fear to only reverent worship can cause us to miss the mark and be misled. So let's draw up the outline, and later we will add the color with the teachings, examples from Scripture, and stories in the chapters ahead. Before we begin, I want to warn you that in defining holy fear you will hear words that could be frightening, but I assure you the opposite is true. Stay with the message through its entirety, and you will discover that holy fear is a gift of love and protection from our Creator, who deeply cares and longs for us.

There are many New Testament scriptures we can start with, but I believe this one sets the tone:

> Therefore, since we are receiving a kingdom which cannot be shaken, let us have grace, by which we may serve God acceptably with *reverence* and *godly fear*. For our God is a consuming fire. (Hebrews 12:28–29 NKJV)

If you look closely, you'll observe there are two terms that are referenced: *reverence* and *godly fear*. This immediately shows that godly fear cannot be limited to only reverence; otherwise, the writer is just repeating himself with the second term. These are not only different words in English but also two different Greek words: *aidōs* and *eulábeia*.

Reverence is an excellent translation of the first Greek word. The *Complete Word Study Dictionary* defines *reverence* as "profound adoring awed respect."[1] I love these four words joined together; stopping to ponder each one takes our understanding to another level!

The second term, *godly fear*, carries the meaning of *awe*. For *awe*'s definition I looked at the original 1828 edition of Noah Webster's dictionary. Here's what I found: "fear, dread inspired by something great and terrific; to strike with fear and reverence. To influence by fear, terror or respect."[2] Don't be alarmed by the words *dread* and *terror*. Though the Greek dictionary also uses these words, remember, holy fear has a drawing, not a repulsive, effect. So we must ask: Is there a positive and healthy aspect of these words? I believe Scripture shows there is, and we'll see this as we add the color later.

Let's begin by listing our definitions. To fear God is to *reverence* and be in complete *awe* of Him.

To fear God is to *hallow* Him. *Hallow* is defined as "to respect greatly."

To fear God is to esteem, respect, honor, venerate, and adore Him above anyone or anything else.

When we fear God, we take on His heart. We love what He loves, and we hate what He hates. (Notice it is not to "dislike" what He hates; rather, it is to "hate" what He hates.) What is important to Him becomes important to us. What is not so important to Him becomes not so important to us.

To fear God is to hate sin.

To fear God is to hate injustice.

To fear God is to depart from evil in every sense—thought, word, and action. It is to refrain from speaking deceitfully. It will not say or put on an appearance that is untrue to one's heart and thoughts. It keeps our outward behavior congruent with our inward thoughts, motives, and beliefs.

To fear God is to walk in authentic humility before God and mankind.

To fear God is to give Him the praise, adoration, thanksgiving, and worship He deserves.

To fear God is to give Him all that belongs to Him.

To fear God is to tremble before Him in wonder and awe. It is to give His Word and presence our full attention.

To fear God is to obey Him. It's not just a desire but an inward force determined to carry out His will, no matter the cost. We eagerly, willingly, and immediately obey—even if we don't see a benefit or it doesn't make sense—and we carry it out to completion.

To fear God is to abstain from any form of complaining, murmuring, or grumbling.

To fear God is to respect, honor, and submit to His direct and delegated authority. It is also to obey the delegated authority, with the only exception being if the authority tells us to sin.

The fear of the Lord shapes our intentions, thoughts, words, and actions.

Now let's partially list the benefits of holy fear. Here are some of the many biblical promises made to those who walk in it.

The fear of the Lord is the starting place for an intimate relationship with God. We become His friends, and His secrets are made known to us.

The fear of the Lord is the beginning of wisdom, understanding, and knowledge. It gives foresight and clear divine direction.

The fear of the Lord is how we mature in our salvation and are conformed to the image of Jesus.

The fear of the Lord is clean; it produces true holiness in our lives.

To abide in the fear of the Lord is to secure an eternal legacy.

The fear of the Lord produces confidence, fearlessness, and security. It swallows up all other fears, including the fear of man.

The fear of the Lord gives us identity, makes us productive, and empowers us to multiply.

The fear of the Lord provides angelic assistance, fulfilled desires, enduring success, nobility, influence, longevity, productive days, enjoyment in life, happiness, pleasure in labor, healing for our body, and so much more.

The fear of the Lord endures forever—it will never fade. The fear of the Lord is a treasured gift from our heavenly Father.

Making It Personal

Passage: Therefore, since we are receiving a kingdom which cannot be shaken, let us have grace, by which we may serve God acceptably with reverence and godly fear. For our God is a consuming fire. (Hebrews 12:28–29 NKJV)

Point: The fear of the Lord is to love what God loves and to hate what God hates. What is important to Him becomes important to us. What is not so important to Him becomes not so important to us.

Ponder: What does it look like, practically, for me to esteem, respect, honor, venerate, and adore God above anyone or anything else?

Prayer: Dear heavenly Father, please teach me how to fear Your name, Word, presence, and all You are. May I love and take pleasure in holy fear. Holy Spirit, as I continue this journey, teach and impart God's ways in me; let what I read not merely be informational, but may the words transform my life into the image of my Lord Jesus Christ. I ask this all in Jesus' name, amen.

Profession: May my words and the meditations of my heart be pleasing in God's sight.

His whole character commands our reverence because it is superlatively holy, and his name is to us a word of awe never to be mentioned flippantly, and never to be quoted without earnest thought and prostration of heart before him.

—C. H. SPURGEON

4 | GOD'S TANGIBLE PRESENCE

As mentioned before, the fear of God seems counterintuitive. When hearing the word *fear*, our minds associate it with a detrimental or even damaging state. But I assure you, the fear of God is actually the greatest force of confidence, comfort, and protection available to any being in the universe. We will discover this truth as we journey onward. But first, holy fear can be broken down into two major categories:

1. to *tremble at the presence of God*, and
2. to *tremble at His Word*.

We will discuss both, but let's begin by highlighting the first. The psalmist declares, "God is *greatly to be feared* in the assembly of the saints, and to be held in *reverence* by all those around Him" (Psalm 89:7 NKJV). Notice it does not state merely "feared" but rather "*greatly*" feared. Here's a firm truth: you will never find God's wonderful presence in an atmosphere where He's not revered and held in awe.

This became reality to me in January 1997. I was asked to speak at a national conference in the capital city of Brazil. I was elated to travel to this great nation for the first time.

The plane landed in Brasilia early in the morning, and I had the day to pray, prepare, and rest in my room. That evening, as we drove to the arena, I couldn't help but notice the numerous vehicles lining the streets before we even arrived. As expected, the parking lot was packed, indicating this conference would be well attended.

I was escorted into the arena, and after meeting a few leaders, I went directly onto the platform. I was ecstatic to worship God with what I anticipated would be thousands of hungry believers. However, my excitement didn't last, as I soon noticed the presence of God was missing from the atmosphere. I was baffled; this was a believers' conference, and the worship team was among the best in the nation, so why the absence of His presence?

Before I continue, let me clarify a few things about God's presence. Scripture identifies two types. The first is His omnipresence. David testifies, "I can never get away from your presence! If I go up to heaven, you are there; if I go down to the grave, you are there . . . Even in darkness I cannot hide from you" (Psalm 139:7–8, 12). This is the presence of God that promises, "I will never leave you nor forsake you" (Hebrews 13:5 NKJV).

The second is identified by Jesus' statement, "I will love him and *manifest* Myself to him" (John 14:21 NKJV). The word *manifest* is the Greek word *emphanízō* and means "to make apparent . . . to let oneself be intimately known and understood." This occurs when God reveals Himself to our mind and senses. Jesus states, "Where two or three are gathered together in My name, I am there in the midst of them" (Matthew 18:20 NKJV). He's obviously not referring to the everywhere-presence of God, because why would He need to make this statement? Rather, He speaks of His manifest presence. This presence was absent in the arena that night. Keenly aware of this, I closed my eyes and asked the Holy Spirit, *Where is Your presence?*

I opened my eyes, and within moments I noticed something I had missed but was now obvious. Most of the people were not engaged in worship. Some, with hands in their pockets or arms crossed across their chest, were gazing around nonchalantly or looking bored. Women fumbled through their purses; many people milled around the auditorium or went out to purchase snacks at the concession stands. Numerous attendees were laughing and talking to one another. Their behavior was no different from a crowd waiting for a show to begin. I thought to myself, *Surely this will cease, and people will engage in worship.* But that wasn't the case.

To my amazement, once the songs of worship were ended and one of the leaders of the movement got up to read from Scripture, nothing changed, except now, with the absence of music, I could hear a low murmur of people engaged in conversation. Anger mounted in my disbelief of what I was witnessing.

I then heard the Spirit of God whisper to my heart, *I want you to directly confront this.*

Once introduced, I walked up to the podium with my translator beside me. I decided not to say anything but only stare at the people. I concluded that the only possible way to get everyone's attention was to cease all activity from the platform. It worked, as a full minute of silence arrested everyone's attention. People's movements ceased, heads turned toward the platform, and the atmosphere fell silent. At this point, I knew every eye was on me in the arena.

I didn't open the evening message with, "It's great to be in Brazil" or "Thank you for having me." Nor did I introduce myself. Rather, I sternly asked this question: "How would you like it if, while you speak to someone sitting across the table, they ignore you, stare at the ceiling as if disinterested, or carry on a conversation with the person next to them?"

After a moment of silence, I answered my own question, "You wouldn't like it, would you?"

I probed further: "What if every time you knock on your neighbor's door you are greeted with a disinterested look along with a monotone voice saying, 'Oh, it's only you.' Would you continue to go to their house?"

Again, after a pause, I answered, "No way!"

I then stated, "Do you think the King of the universe is going to manifest His presence or speak in a place where He is not honored and revered?"

This time I answered the question firmly: "Never!"

I continued, "If the president of your nation stood on this platform, he would have been granted your full attention and respect. Or if one of your favorite soccer players stood here, most of you would be on the edge of your seats with excitement, anticipating every word. Yet while God's Word was being read a moment ago, you paid no attention to it; it was white noise to you!"

I then spoke to the people for the next ninety minutes on the fear of the Lord. You could hear a pin drop. It seemed they were a bit stunned by the confrontation but nevertheless listened intently.

Once finished, I gave the call, "If you are a believer, but you lack holy fear, and you are willing to repent, stand up!"

Without hesitation, 75 percent of the people stood to their feet. Within moments, before praying with them, the manifest presence of God filled the arena. People started sobbing and crying as the wonderful presence of God touched their lives. The holy fear did not scare them away from God; it drew them in close.

What happened next is one of the most awesome experiences I've had in forty years of ministry. But before we get to that story, let's close with these words:

When I heard the sound of his voice, I *fainted* and lay there with my face to the ground. Just then a hand touched me and lifted me, *still trembling*, to my hands and knees. And the man said to me, "Daniel, *you are very precious to God*, so listen carefully to what I have to say to you. Stand up, for I have been sent to you." When he said this to me, I stood up, *still trembling*. (Daniel 10:9–11)

Daniel was very precious to God, yet he was overwhelmed and fell to the ground. Even as he was assisted to his knees, then to his feet, he trembled the entire time. If this happens in the presence of a messenger—an angel—what happens when God Himself comes?

Making It Personal

Passage: God is greatly to be feared in the assembly of the saints, and to be held in reverence by all those around Him. (Psalm 89:7 NKJV)

Point: We will only find God's manifest presence in an atmosphere where He's held with the utmost respect.

Ponder: What does it mean to tremble at God's presence? How is this practically lived out when I'm alone? When I'm with friends? When I'm in public places? When I'm in a church service?

Prayer: Dear heavenly Father, I ask Your forgiveness for the times I've entered an atmosphere of worship with a casual, irreverent attitude. I repent for taking Your presence for granted, for treating it as common. May the blood of Jesus cleanse me. I humble myself before You and ask for grace to change. I want to be aware of and respect Your presence no matter where I am or what I'm doing. I want to live in reverent awe of You at all times. I ask this in Jesus' name, amen.

Profession: I will always give full attention to God's Word and honor His presence in all I say and do.

*Before prayer, endeavor
to realize Whose Presence
you are approaching and
to Whom you are about
to speak, keeping in mind
Whom you are addressing.*

—TERESA OF AVILA

5 | AN UNFORGETTABLE EVENING

The gospel of Mark testifies of the Lord working with the disciples, "confirming the word through the accompanying signs" (Mark 16:20 NKJV). This joint venture began once Jesus ascended to heaven, and nowhere in the New Testament are we told that it would cease before His return.

So let's return to that evening in Brazil. When the call was given to repent of irreverence, 75 percent of the people stood to their feet. I bowed my head and prayed aloud, "Lord God, confirm Your Word proclaimed tonight."

Within moments I heard sobbing among the people. For the next few minutes, a wave of God's presence filled the atmosphere, refreshing and cleansing the hearts of those in attendance. Even after it subsided, a wonderful peace lingered.

The people hadn't verbally asked for forgiveness or prayed, yet God's presence manifested due to their changed hearts. In pondering this later, I realized the prodigal son's father didn't wait to hear his son ask for forgiveness before running to him. No, it was merely the son's change of heart coupled with his corresponding action of coming home that drew an enthusiastic embrace and kiss from his father. It seemed the same was happening in this arena.

We were in a special moment; the people were in the place of reverent silence and tenderheartedness. It seemed good to lead them in a prayer of repentance, and it didn't take a lot of discernment to recognize their words were sincere and heartfelt. Moments after praying, another wave of God's manifest presence flooded the arena. Once more I could hear sobs and weeping among the people, but more intense this time. It was truly beautiful, yet it lifted again after a few minutes.

I was grateful for the refreshing we all sensed from two manifestations of God's peaceful and wonderful presence. We all stayed in a place of expectancy as a divine tranquility permeated the atmosphere. In the stillness, I heard the Spirit of God whisper to my heart, *I'm going to manifest one more time.*

I uttered aloud what I heard; however, none of us was aware of what would happen next—a different presence was about to meet us. It's difficult to share what happened, for words cannot do it justice. What I'm about to write will seemed far-fetched, even unrealistic, but for more than twenty years afterward, numerous people have confirmed what took place.

Imagine standing in a forest when a strong windstorm blows in. You hear the loud whistling of the wind through the trees above you. This is similar to the sound of the wind that blew through the arena. We couldn't feel it, but we heard it. Almost simultaneously those in attendance erupted in fervent prayers and cries. Their voices thundered, yet the sound of the wind overpowered the level of their voices. I was stunned, in awe, and almost terrified by His presence. I couldn't move, couldn't speak, and there were goose bumps all over my body. There was an authority in the atmosphere like nothing I'd ever encountered. I thought, *This isn't the presence of Abba Father; it is our holy, awesome, mighty King!*[1]

The roar of the wind lasted around ninety seconds. As it gradually subsided, it left in its wake people weeping, some passed out, some collapsed over the seat back in front of them—but all of us were trembling in awe. The solemn aftermath continued for another ten minutes or so. I couldn't say anything; we all remained still and silent. I then turned the service over to the leader and was escorted quietly back to the car.

That evening's featured soloist and her husband got in our car a few moments after me. Immediately, she cried out, "Did you hear the wind?"

I didn't want to go straight to acknowledging it. I wanted someone other than me to confirm what actually happened. So I responded, "Maybe it was a low-flying jet plane over the building." (This entire arena had a gap between the upper wall and ceiling to create air ventilation, so you could hear sounds coming from outside much easier than a closed-in structure.)

She sat in the front seat, turned with a look of shock on her face, and passionately countered, "No, it was the Spirit of God!"

Her husband, who was a quieter man, interjected, "Sir, that was no jet airplane."

I asked, "How do you know?"

He responded, "There were security personnel and policemen outside the arena, many of them not believers. When they heard the sound of the wind, they came rushing in and asked our team about the sound of the loud blowing wind coming from inside the building. Furthermore, I was at the main sound board [he was there to make sure the sound levels were correct for his wife's time of singing]. Not one bit of the sound came through the sound system; the decibel meters registered nothing the entire time the wind blew."

His wife continued with tears streaming down her face, "I saw waves of fire falling in the building and I could sense angels everywhere."

I asked to be taken straight to my hotel. We were silent on the ride there. Later that evening, I sat on the balcony of my room for hours; all I could do was worship God. I was overwhelmed by what had taken place that evening.

The next morning, when we entered the auditorium, the atmosphere was completely different. The manifest presence of God that had impacted us during the previous night's service was still notable. The fear of God had been restored in the hearts of the people, and they were experiencing His presence and blessings in a wonderful way.

As already stated, several have since confirmed what transpired that evening and have shared the impact on their lives through mail, emails, and in person. In 2016, I traveled to speak to twelve thousand leaders in Goiânia, Brazil. The welcoming pastor's first words to me as he shook my hand were, "I was in the meeting in Brasilia twenty years ago when the wind blew. My life has never been the same since." He is a leader in a church network that grew to over 300,000 people in just sixteen years.

When my wife was in Brazil in 2019 to minister at a conference, one of the leaders of a different movement reported being in the service where the wind blew more than twenty years earlier. She, too, reported that her life had been forever changed.

Being in God's presence is crucial to the spiritual health of every believer. It used to be very difficult for me to enter God's presence in my times of prayer. But one day I started doing something, practically by accident. I decided not to begin my time of prayer singing or uttering any words. I merely pondered the awesomeness and holiness of our God. Almost immediately I was met with His presence. I decided to do the same the next day and experienced the same result. And on the third day, it happened again.

I was baffled. I asked, "Lord, why is it so easy for me the past three days to get into Your presence?"

I heard the Spirit of God say, *How did Jesus teach His disciples to pray?*

I started quoting the Lord's Prayer: "Our Father in heaven, *hallowed* be Your name . . ." I yelled out, "That's it! Jesus taught His disciples to come into the presence of God with holy awe and reverence!" It now made total sense to me.

David confirms this truth by stating, "*In fear of You* I will worship toward Your holy temple" (Psalm 5:7 NKJV). God is our Father, Jesus is our Lord and Savior, and the Spirit of God loves us deeply. But also remember, in the New Testament, God is called "the consuming fire" (Hebrews 12:29). Jesus caused John, the beloved apostle who was closest to Him, to fall on his face as a dead man (Revelation 1:17), and the Spirit of God is the One who manifests the might of God to get the attention of an entire city (Acts 2), shake buildings (Acts 4), and do many other awesome acts.

Here is the bottom-line truth: *where the Lord is reverenced, His presence manifests.*

========================== **Making It Personal** ==========================

Passage: I was with you . . . in fear, and in much trembling. And my speech and my preaching were not with persuasive words of human wisdom, but in demonstration of the Spirit and of power, that your faith should not be in the wisdom of men but in the power of God. (1 Corinthians 2:3–5 NKJV)

Point: The fear of the Lord changes atmospheres. It cultivates an environment for the Holy Spirit's power to change our lives and the lives of others.

Ponder: Have I expected and believed for God's presence and power to manifest? How will my prayer life change by approaching Him with holy awe? How can I make this shift?

Prayer: Dear heavenly Father, if I've restricted the manifestation of Your presence due to past experiences or have been influenced by others' limitations of what You can do, please forgive me. I will enter Your presence in holy awe and place no restrictions on You. Please exceed what I can ask, think, or hope for in revealing Your power. Please do this to glorify my Lord Jesus and minister to the people in my world of influence. I ask this in Jesus' name, amen.

Profession: All things are possible if I only believe and approach God with holy fear.

When we see Him face-to-face in all His awesome holiness and blazing glory, it will seem incredible to us that we ever had a casual thought in relation to Him.

—JOY DAWSON

6 | BEHOLDING HIM

Our holy fear grows proportionally to our comprehension of God's greatness. Yet here is the reality: "No one can measure his greatness" (Psalm 145:3) because His glory is beyond understanding. His glory is unsearchable, has no boundaries, no limitations, and is incomparable. Even so, we should seek to increase our comprehension.

In the year Judah's King Uzziah passed away, approximately 742 BC, the prophet Isaiah was transported to heaven. He saw the Lord seated on His throne, highly exalted, in all His glory. His awesomeness filled the massive arena, a structure that most likely could hold more than a billion beings.

Not only was Isaiah astounded and overwhelmed by the Creator, but he was enamored by the mighty angels called seraphim hovering over God's throne. From the lips of these awe-inspiring beings Isaiah heard:

"Holy, holy, holy is the LORD of Heaven's Armies! The whole earth is filled with his glory!" (Isaiah 6:3)

Many of us are familiar with the classic hymn "Holy, Holy, Holy," containing these same words and written in the 1800s by John Bacchus Dykes.

It's been a staple chorus in the church for over two hundred years and consequently branded as a soft melody of worship. However, this was far from what Isaiah witnessed.

These massive beings are not singing a lovely song to make God feel good about Himself; rather, they are responding to what they see! Fresh new facets of His unsearchable greatness are continuously being revealed, and all they can do is cry out, "Holy, holy, holy . . ."

The seraphim don't repeat "holy" three times. When a Hebrew writer, such as Isaiah, sought to emphasize a word, it would be written twice. We see this in Jesus' statement, "Not everyone who says to Me, 'Lord, Lord,' shall enter the kingdom of heaven" (Matthew 7:21 NKJV). If you were Matthew sitting and listening to Jesus, you would have noticed significant amplification to His voice when He got to the word *Lord*. To capture His emphasis, Matthew wrote it twice. In the English language, we use bold face or italic type to convey emphasis.

Very rarely does a Hebrew writer elevate the word to the third degree of emphasis. In fact, it only happens a couple times in Scripture. This would give the word or statement the highest degree of emphasis. In essence, these angels' voices thunder to such a degree that it shakes the doorposts of this massive arena.

When our family moved to Florida, we discovered there were no basements due to the water table being too high. Our home builder informed me, "If a tornado threatens your neighborhood, get under the doorjambs of an interior room of your house because it's the most stable part of the structure." It's mind-blowing to think Isaiah specifically identified the doorjambs shaking in this massive heavenly arena. This being so, it's probable the entire structure was rumbling from these mighty angels' shouts!

What was Isaiah's response in beholding the Lord's glory? It wasn't, "Wow, there He is!"

No, he cried out, "It's all over! I am doomed, for I am a sinful man. I have filthy lips" (Isaiah 6:5). Consider this reality: This is a godly man—a prophet—one who cries out in the previous chapter of his book, "Woe to those who call evil good, and good evil, woe to those who are proud, woe to those who are drunkards!" (Isaiah 5:20–22, author's paraphrase). Yet now, one chapter later, he has one glimpse of God's greatness, and his cry is no longer "woe to the sinners"; rather it's "Woe is me, for I am undone!" (6:5 NKJV). He thought he knew, but now he's much more aware of who Almighty God is. He is also well aware of who he is before this holy God. What resulted from this encounter? His holy fear increased by many levels!

We see similar responses throughout Scripture with those who behold the Lord in His glory. How about Job? The Almighty says about him, "'Have you noticed my servant Job? He is the finest man in all the earth'" (Job 1:8). Can you imagine God saying this about you or me? We would be jumping up and down with joy! Yet this man encounters God's glory and cries out, "'I have heard of You by the hearing of the ear, but now my eye sees You. Therefore I abhor myself'" (Job 42:5–6 NKJV).

How about Ezekiel? He saw the Lord and wrote, "This is what the glory of the LORD looked like to me. When I saw it, I fell face down on the ground" (Ezekiel 1:28).

Or what about Abraham? We read that when he saw God, "Abram fell face down on the ground" (Genesis 17:3).

When God gloriously manifested on Sinai, "Moses himself was so frightened at the sight that he said, 'I am terrified and trembling'" (Hebrews 12:21).

John the apostle, the one Jesus loved, writes of his encounter with our glorified Jesus, "When I saw him, I fell at his feet as if I were dead" (Revelation 1:17).

The above is not an exhaustive list. There are many other similar incidents recorded in Scripture.

More recently in church history, around 1266 to 1273, Thomas Aquinas was writing Summa Theologica, which he considered to be his most important work. But one day he encountered God so powerfully that it changed his perspective forever—and he stop writing altogether. His friend Reginald urged him to keep going, but Aquinas responded, "The end of my labours is come. All that I have written appears to be straw after what's been revealed to me."[1]

At one point in Israel's history, God seeks to upgrade His people's holy fear by asking some pointed questions. Isaiah, who beheld the Lord's glory, asks, "Who is able to advise the Spirit of the LORD? Who knows enough to give him advice or teach him? Has the LORD ever needed anyone's advice? Does he need instruction about what is good? . . . To whom can you compare God? What image can you find to resemble him?" (Isaiah 40:13–14, 18).

Then God directly asks: "'To whom will you compare me? Who is my equal?'" (Isaiah 40:25).

If there has ever been a time in history that these questions should be deeply pondered and not just skimmed over, it's now. In this day and hour, many of us are so preoccupied with the onslaught of information that continually fills our minds that we don't have the space or time to meditate on these crucial questions. Our development of holy fear has been hindered, and consequently many believers are vulnerable and easily drawn into the world's system of desire, gain, and the pride of human achievements.

In similar fashion, we are continually bombarded by the accolades of talented athletes, beautiful Hollywood stars, gifted musical artists, business gurus, charismatic leaders, and other important individuals. Their fame is lauded on television, social media, mainstream media, and many other public platforms. The tragic reality is that these seemingly harmless snippets of information and human achievements distract us or even pull us away from the magnificent invitation to draw near and behold Him.[1]

If we would just pause, turn inward, and gaze at His magnificence, we would be enriched, strengthened, and at peace. We are promised:

> For God, who said, "Let there be light in the darkness," has made this light shine in our hearts so we could know the glory of God that is seen in the face of Jesus Christ. (2 Corinthians 4:6)

In the stillness of our souls, in union with the Holy Spirit, we can behold

---

1. See appendix A for more in-depth discussion.

Jesus as we ponder His Word. Gazing into His face illuminates God's glory in our hearts and subsequently causes our *holy awe* to level up. We become like Isaiah and the other greats listed above who encountered Him, walked with Him, pleased Him, received covenant promises, and finished well. Best of all, in beholding Him we are promised to be made "more and more like him as we are changed into his glorious image" (2 Corinthians 3:18).

Whose image do you aspire to be conformed to—the celebrities of our day, or the One who created the universe? Choose wisely, and take heed to what you hear and give your attention to.

Making It Personal

Passage: Worship the LORD in all his holy splendor. Let all the earth tremble before him. (Psalm 96:9)

Point: Our holy fear grows proportionally to our comprehension of God's greatness.

Ponder: What would happen if I took ten-minute segments three times a day, shut out all outside influences, and pondered the greatness of God? Is it worth investing the time? Could I be more effective in daily life by increasing my holy fear, which ultimately will make me wiser?

Prayer: Dear heavenly Father, I ask that You grant me a fresh vision of Jesus. Your Word promises that as I behold Him in my heart, I will be transformed into His image, from one level of glory to another. May my holy fear increase as His glory becomes more real. I ask this in Jesus' name, amen.

Profession: I am being transformed into the image of Jesus from glory to glory.

Men reverence one
another, not yet God.

—HENRY DAVID THOREAU

7 | THE GLORY OF GOD

You cannot have a conversation about holy fear without focusing on the *glory of God*. We touched on it in our previous chapter, but now let's take it further.

Mortal flesh cannot stand in the presence of God's glory. The prophet Habakkuk declares it to be "as brilliant as the sunrise. Rays of light flash from his hands, where his awesome power is hidden" (3:4). Paul writes that Jesus dwells in "*unapproachable light*, whom no man has seen or can see" (1 Timothy 6:16 NKJV). Along these same lines, the writer of Hebrews tells us that *God is a consuming fire* (12:29).

Upon hearing these statements, don't think of a wood-burning fire, which consumes yet is still approachable. Let's instead consider a brighter, consuming fire—how about the sun that lights our world? It's consuming and unapproachable, but even that example falls far short, for we are also told, "God is light and in Him is no darkness at all" (1 John 1:5 NKJV). The sun, as bright as it is, has dark spots. In fact, Paul writes, "At midday, O king, along the road I saw a light from heaven, brighter than the sun, shining around me" (Acts 26:13 NKJV).

Paul does not see Jesus' actual face; he only sees the light emanating from Him, and it overwhelms the bright Middle Eastern sun! It is not the morning or late-afternoon sun, rather the noonday sun.

I've traveled extensively to numerous places all over the earth. Occasionally, I forget to bring my sunglasses. In most locations, I can get along without them; however, not in the Middle East. On my first visit there, I discovered the necessity of sunglasses; without them I had to continually squint my eyes to mere cracks due to the effects of the sun. It's much brighter there for three reasons: the dry desert climate, the light color and reflective nature of the terrain, and being located near the equator. Although it wasn't too intense early or later in the day, at midday it seemed blinding without protective lenses.

Now let's ponder what we just read. Paul states that the light emanating from Jesus is brighter than the noontime Middle Eastern sun! His glory exceeds the sun's brilliance many times.

This explains why both Joel and Isaiah say that the sun and moon will be darkened and the stars will not shine on the day Jesus returns (Isaiah 13:9–10; Joel 2:31–32). Allow me to elaborate. When we walk out on a clear night, what do we see? A sky full of stars. But what happens when the sun comes up in the morning? The stars disappear. We must ask, do all the stars quickly run away as the sun rises, and then, when the sun goes down, do the stars suddenly run back out in the night sky? The answer to that question is obviously no. What happens? The glory of the stars is one level, but the glory of the sun is a much greater level. So, when the sun comes out, because it is so much brighter than the stars, it darkens them.

When Jesus returns, His glory will be so much greater than the sun, He will darken it, even though it will still be burning! Are you getting a better glimpse of His glory? I believe this is why we are told that all the people of the earth are going to cry out "to the mountains and the rocks, 'Fall on us and *hide us from the face* of the one who sits on the throne and from the wrath of the Lamb!'" (Revelation 6:16).

So now the main question: What is the glory of the Lord? To answer that, let's go to Moses' request: "Please, show me Your *glory*" (Exodus 33:18 NKJV).

The Hebrew word for *glory* is *kabod*. Strong's Bible dictionary defines it as "the weight of something." It also speaks of majesty and honor. So Moses is asking, "Show me Yourself in *all* your splendor." Look carefully at God's response:

> "I will make all My *goodness* pass before you, and I will *proclaim the name of the* LORD before you." (Exodus 33:19 NKJV)

God identifies Moses' request for glory as "all My *goodness*." The Hebrew word for *goodness* is defined as "good in the widest sense." In other words, nothing is withheld.

Next God says, "I will proclaim the name of the LORD before you." Before an earthly king enters his throne room, a herald first proclaims his name. The trumpets blow, and the king enters the throne room in all his splendor. The king's greatness is revealed, and in his court, there is no mistake as to who the king is. However, if this monarch were casually strolling down the street of his large nation dressed in ordinary clothes, without any attendants, he might be passed by without recognition.

We learned in the previous chapter the glory of the Lord is revealed in the face of Jesus Christ. Many have claimed to experience a vision of Jesus. That is very possible, but not in His full glory. Paul describes it this way: "For now we see through a glass, darkly; but then face to face" (1 Corinthians 13:12 KJV). His glory is hidden, even as it was veiled by a dark cloud in the Old Testament. Why? No flesh can look upon His unveiled glory and still live.

The first person Jesus spoke with after His resurrection was Mary Magdalene, yet she thought He was the gardener (John 20:15–16). The disciples ate a fish breakfast with Jesus along the seashore, but at first they didn't recognize Him (John 21:9–10). Two disciples walked with Jesus on the road to Emmaus, "but their eyes were restrained" (Luke 24:16 NKJV). These all beheld His face because He did not openly display His glory.

There were some who saw the Lord in the Old Testament, but He was not revealed in His glory. The Lord appeared to Abraham by the terebinth trees of Mamre, but not in His glory (Genesis 18:1–2). Jacob wrestled with God, but not in His glory (Genesis 32:24–30). Joshua, when near Jericho, saw the Lord with a drawn sword and demanded to know if He was on Israel's side. Upon learning it was the Lord, he fell to his face and worshipped Him. The list continues with Gideon, Samson's parents, and many others.

In contrast, John the apostle saw the Lord, in the Spirit, in all His glory on the island of Patmos. John compared His countenance to the sun shining in its strength and fell as one dead. How could John look at Him? He was not in his body, but in the spirit. The same is true for Isaiah and a few others. Moses, on the other hand, could not look upon God's face, for Moses was in his mortal body.

The glory of the Lord is everything that makes God, God. All His characteristics, authority, power, wisdom—literally the immeasurable weight and magnitude of God. Nothing is hidden or held back! This is the One who put the stars in their place with His fingers and gave every one of them a name. He's the One who measured the entire universe with His fingers—the span of His hand. The One who can pick up the whole earth as if it were a grain of sand; He weighed every drop of water in the palm of His hand; He weighed the earth and the mountains in His scales. This is the One we can behold in our hearts and subsequently change into His image, from glory to glory!

This is the One who deeply loves us—so much so, He chose to pay the terrible judgment for our sins so we could be a part of His family. I don't know about you, but this really excites me!

Making It Personal

Passage: He who is the blessed and only Potentate, the King of kings and Lord of lords, who alone has immortality, dwelling in unapproachable light, whom no man has seen or can see, to whom be honor and everlasting power. Amen. (1 Timothy 6:15–16 NKJV)

Point: The glory of the Lord is everything that makes God, God. All His characteristics, authority, power, wisdom—literally the immeasurable weight and magnitude of God. Nothing is hidden or held back!

Ponder: Imagine a light so brilliant and pure that no darkness, shadows, dullness, or dimming can be present. Imagine this light shining in my heart. Why would I ever think about or ever want to hide anything from Him? It's impossible.

Prayer: Dear heavenly Father, I ask that You give me keen awareness of Your glory. I don't want this to be a trivial reality, a casual thing, or something that I periodically think of; rather I want its magnitude to become ever present and more real than the world that surrounds me. May Your glory be before my heart and mind continually. I ask this in Jesus' name, amen.

Profession: In Christ, I am the light of the world, reflecting His glory to all whom I encounter.

Revealed
As We Are

WEEK 2

We must fear God out of love,
not love Him out of fear.

—SAINT FRANCIS DE SALES

8 | YOUR VALUE

This section will include some weighty and possibly convicting topics. So before continuing, let's pause and deepen our understanding of God's tremendous love for us. I'll open with a strong, almost frightening, statement from Jesus, which will be a significant part of our dialog in this section. If not read in context, His words could be misunderstood—and possibly instill unhealthy fear—so I implore you to read them with a heart of submission and reverence toward our God:

> I'll tell you whom to fear. *Fear God*, who has the power to kill you and then throw you into hell. Yes, he's the one *to fear.* (Luke 12:5)

Jesus tells us to *fear God*—and He doesn't just say it once; He emphasizes this directive by repeating it. The real attention-grabber is His startling words, "throw you into hell." That is strong language! However, look at His very next statement:

> Are not five sparrows sold for two copper coins? And not one of them is forgotten before God. But the very hairs of your head are all numbered. *Do not fear* therefore; you are of more *value* than many sparrows. (Luke 12:6–7 NKJV)

47

Notice I've highlighted "Fear God" in verse 5 and "Do not fear" in verse 7. Once again, we see a differentiation of *holy fear* and *unholy fear*. I cannot stress enough that holy fear does not mean being scared of God and consequently withdrawing from Him, but *unholy* fear does. It's imperative that we know the difference and are established in this truth.

Jesus opens with a gripping, almost terrifying, statement, yet in the same breath He declares our inconceivable *value* to God. In essence, He reveals that God deeply treasures us and, therefore, grants us the gift of holy fear. This gift safeguards us by keeping us close to the Giver of life and away from what would ruin us: *the fear of man*, which is the polar opposite of holy fear. The two will be a significant part our discussion moving forward, but before embarking, we'll first discuss our *value*.

According to Jesus, God so deeply cherishes you that He knows the number of hairs on your head. Science estimates most humans have on average 100,000 hairs on their scalp. If you put 10,000 people in a room, do you think you could determine which one has 99,569 hairs? Even if you guessed correctly, you'd be wrong in minutes because the average person loses 50 to 100 hairs per day. God knows our exact number at any given moment! What does this tell us? We're so valued, He thinks about us continuously. David writes:

> How precious also are Your thoughts to me, O God! How great is the sum of them! If I should count them, they would be more in number than the sand. (Psalm 139:17–18 NKJV)

All the sand! Think of all the sand on earth—every beach, desert, and golf course. That's an enormous amount! Science and math enthusiasts tell us that depending on the size and how tightly packed, there are approximately five hundred million to a billion granules of sand in one cubic square foot of beach.[1] Our minds would struggle to comprehend the vast number of granules on just the Florida beaches. But think of it—if you add up all the granules of sand on the planet, you still wouldn't have the number of thoughts God has about you!

Ask yourself this question: What do you predominantly think of? You rarely think about something you don't value. Lisa and I have items that I discover every year when I go to our storage locker at Christmastime. I use the term *discover* because I forget we own them. I don't think of these items once the entire year because they're not valuable. However, if I numbered all my thoughts of Lisa over our forty years of marriage, I might get the amount of sand filling half a shoe box. That's approximately two hundred million thoughts, which would amount to a thought every 6.3 seconds. A husband who thinks of his wife that often would be considered one deeply in love with her.

God's thoughts about you outnumber every grain of sand on the planet! Are you comprehending this? Here is what's astounding: God cannot exaggerate! Though we've all been around people who have exaggerated and made statements far from the truth, God cannot stray one iota from truth; He cannot tell a lie. So in stating that His thoughts about you outnumber every grain of sand on the planet, that's huge!

Let's take it further. What exactly is our value? Value is determined by the purchaser. My son attended a sports auction because his company was interested in buying a Bill Russell jersey worn in a championship game in the 1960s. They passed on the purchase because the highest bid came in at $1,044,000! As great a player as Bill Russell was, I personally wouldn't have given over a couple hundred dollars for his jersey or any other NBA player's uniform. It is just a piece of clothing.

The question is not about what our value is to people, because that varies. And furthermore, the world does not have a great track record of valuing people as we should. Millions of babies have been murdered in their mothers' wombs. Did people value the lives of those babies? And what about girls and women who are trafficked for sex, including prostitutes? If measured by the people who put them there, their value has been reduced to a few hundred dollars.

God is the One who sets the real measure of worth in this universe, not man. And even for those things we esteem, Jesus reminds us that "what people value highly is detestable in God's sight" (Luke 16:15 NIV). He also makes this remarkable statement: "What profit is it to a man if he gains the whole world, and loses his own soul? Or what will a man give in exchange for his soul?" (Matthew 16:26 NKJV).

Consider for a moment all the wealth of the world. Consider the multi-million-dollar mansions, beautiful properties, gems, precious metals, fine cars, yachts, and planes. It's almost unimaginable. Recent studies estimate the gross world product to be $84.97 trillion. That is an inconceivable amount of money. Yet Jesus tells us that if you were to exchange your life for all of it, you have made an unprofitable deal!

So what is your value? Paul writes, "God bought you with a high price" (1 Corinthians 6:20). God's bid for you—His set price—is found in these words: "For God so loved the world that He *gave* His only begotten Son" (John 3:16 NKJV). Wow, that's a whole lot more than Bill Russell's jersey! God saw our value as equal to His most prized possession. Here is the amazing truth: If we had been worth one penny less to God than the value of Jesus, then this exchange wouldn't have been made, for God would not make an unprofitable deal—to give something more valuable for something less valuable. Are you grasping how precious you are to God?

How enormous is God's love for you? Jesus makes the most startling statement in a prayer:

"The world will know that you [God] sent me [Jesus Christ] and that you love them *as much* as you love me." (John 17:23)

This is almost too much to comprehend! God loves you as much as He loves Jesus! Still, you may think, *He is only speaking of the disciples*. That is incorrect, for Jesus clarifies, "I am praying not only for these disciples but also for all who will ever believe in me through their message" (John 17:20). If you believe in Jesus Christ, you do so either directly or indirectly from the disciples' testimony. The depth of God's love and the value He places on you is incomprehensible.

With this truth firmly established, let's continue to unpack why this gift of holy fear is so crucial in our relationship with Him.

Making It Personal

Passage: They cannot redeem themselves from death by paying a ransom to God. Redemption does not come so easily, for no one can ever pay enough to live forever. (Psalm 49:7–9)

Point: No wise person will make an unprofitable deal—to give what is more valuable for that which is less valuable. In the same way, God would never make an unprofitable deal. The price God paid for you was the life of His only begotten Son, which means He values you as much as He values Jesus. It also means He values those around you as much as He values Jesus.

Ponder: Considering the great value Jesus has placed on my life, how do I now view myself? How does this affect how I view and treat those I encounter daily?

Prayer: Dear heavenly Father, thank You for esteeming my life as so valuable that You were willing to give Jesus to die in my place. Jesus, thank You for esteeming me even better than Yourself by taking my place and taking my judgment. Holy Spirit, I ask that You give me the firm realization in my heart and mind of how much You love and value me, and may I love others the same. In Jesus' name, amen.

Profession: I will love and value others in the same way God loves and values me.

When we preach the love of God there is a danger of forgetting that the Bible reveals not first the love of God but the intense, blazing holiness of God, with His love at the center of that holiness.

—OSWALD CHAMBERS

9 | THE FATAL COLLISION

In the first section we discussed the glory of God, and we only skimmed the surface. In this chapter we'll focus on the various magnitudes of God's presence. Let's start by going to a time period when the Almighty chose to dwell in a tent—when the nation of Israel dwelled in the wilderness.

After time-consuming, elaborate, and intricate work, the tabernacle was completed by a team of laborers. It was constructed according to the exact plan God gave to Moses on the mountain and was a rough model of the heavenly tabernacle (Hebrews 8:1–5). Once the work was finished, God manifested His glorious presence:

> Then the cloud covered the Tabernacle, and the glory of the LORD filled the Tabernacle. Moses could no longer enter. (Exodus 40:34–35)

Once again, God shielded Israel from His glory with a dark cloud. He would dwell with His beloved people in a manner they could endure. Only the high priest was permitted once a year, by the blood of animals, to enter the Most Holy Place. This position was divinely selected, and the first was Aaron, Moses' brother.

On a certain day two of Aaron's sons, who were also priests, entered the tabernacle to offer *"profane fire before the* LORD, which He had not commanded them" (Leviticus 10:1 NKJV). There are differing opinions as to the specifics of what actually happened, but for the sake of getting to the heart of the matter, let's bypass their actions and focus on their motive. One definition of *profane* is "to treat something sacred with irreverence." It means to treat what is holy as common or ordinary. In essence, Aaron's sons came into the glorious presence of God with irreverence. What happens next is sobering, and even frightening:

> So fire blazed forth from the LORD's presence and burned them up, and they died there before the LORD. (Leviticus 10:2)

These two men, who were authorized to come into God's presence, immediately died for their irreverence. Did God viciously attack them? No, they put themselves in harm's way. Think of it this way: The earth is 93,000,000 miles from the sun. To sunbathe at the beach for most is delightful, but if your sunbathing takes place inside 10,000 miles of the same sun, you will meet immediate death.

They erred in becoming too familiar with God's holy and glorious presence and consequently acted in a way that brought disaster upon them. Listen to the words Moses straightaway spoke to Aaron after his sons' deaths:

> "This is what the LORD spoke, saying: 'By those who come near Me I must be regarded as holy; and before all the people I must be glorified.'" (Leviticus 10:3 NKJV)

What Moses stated is a universal and eternal decree. *Universal* means that it applies to every created being, whether human or angelic. *Eternal* implies what has always been will always be—it's never going to change. You can only come into His presence with a heart and attitude of reverence.

Let's think back to my evening in Brazil. In the awesome presence of God while the wind blew, I was paralyzed with holy fear. The thought that literally pulsated through my mind was, *John Bevere, you make one wrong move, you say one wrong word, and you are a dead man!*

Would this actually have happened? I don't know for sure, but what I can say for certain is that a man and woman in the New Testament made a wrong move in a similar atmosphere and they both fell over dead. Yes, the "dead" that constitutes being buried six feet underground (Acts 5:1–10). This couple brought an offering before their church leaders and fellow believers. Yet they both were instantly killed and buried the same day. When this happened, how did the other believers react?

> So *great fear* came upon all the church and upon all who heard these things. (Acts 5:11 NKJV)

A couple things to note. It doesn't say that "great fear came to the city." No, it reads, "great fear came upon all the church." Second, notice it doesn't only say "fear," but "great fear." Hebrew writers didn't exaggerate as we often do in Western culture. By Scripture stating "great," it's a very strong magnitude of holy fear.

In Acts 2, when the Spirit of God initially manifested on the day of Pentecost, some of those who stood by concluded the disciples were drunk on wine at nine o'clock in the morning. Stop and ponder how an inebriated person behaves. It isn't usually quiet and reserved; rather, most often, it's a lot of laughter and joy. This describes the atmosphere on that notable day. Our loving God's presence was refreshing and delightful. But when His awesome, even terrifying, presence manifested for judgment in the midst of the same people, the church was gripped with great fear and awe. This event dramatically increased their awareness of God's holiness.

I've often been asked, "Why haven't people fallen over dead in modern times?" It's a good and valid question. This couple lied to Peter and, ultimately, the Holy Spirit. There have been plenty of pastors lied to in the twenty-first century, so why haven't the offenders met the same fate? Let's look at what happens immediately after this couple's death:

> They brought the sick out into the streets and laid them on beds and couches, that at least the shadow of Peter passing by might fall on some of them . . . and they were all healed. (Acts 5:15–16 NKJV)

This is mind-boggling when you think it through. Notice it was the streets (plural)! And it was not "some" but "all" who were healed! Let's modernize this. It would be as if the apostle Peter entered a major hospital and cleared out every bed on every floor by just walking down the hallways. This magnitude of power is found only in the atmosphere of the Lord's glory.

Let's further confirm this with another scriptural example. Hundreds of years after the incident with Aaron's two sons, another set of sons who were also priests, Hophni and Phinehas, were committing adultery with the women who assembled at the door of the same tabernacle. This would be less than ninety feet from where Aaron's sons had died on the spot! If that weren't enough, they were also intimidating the worshippers by forcefully taking offerings. They were "scoundrels who had no respect for the LORD or for their duties as priests" (1 Samuel 2:12–13). God said of these men, "I have vowed that the sins of Eli and his sons will never be forgiven" (1 Samuel 3:14). You never want to hear these words from the mouth of Almighty God!

Their behavior was extremely offensive to God, several degrees more irreverent than Aaron's sons, yet these men did not instantly die at the same tabernacle. Why? The answer is found in these words: "The word of the LORD was rare in those days; *there was* no widespread revelation" (1 Samuel 3:1 NKJV). The lack of God's revealed Word speaks to the absence of His presence; it was nonexistent, no different than the worship service in Brazil. However, in the days of Moses it was fully present.

What conclusion can we draw from these examples? The greater God's manifest glory, the greater and swifter the judgment of irreverence. Therefore, *delayed judgment is not denied judgment.* For this reason, Paul writes:

> Some men's sins are clearly evident, preceding them to judgment, but those of some men follow later. (1 Timothy 5:24 NKJV)

It is wise never to permit under any circumstances an irreverent, casual, or familiar attitude toward God. It's actually more dangerous when His glory is not manifesting. Why? It's easier to slip into a state of irreverence from the deceptive belief of being accepted due to the lack of judgment. If this occurs, we can easily slip into the belief that God doesn't care about our irreverence, as we will see in the next chapter.

Making It Personal

Passage: "By those who come near Me I must be regarded as holy; and before all the people I must be glorified." (Leviticus 10:3 NKJV)

Point: The greater God's manifest glory, the greater and swifter the judgment of irreverence. Therefore, delayed judgment is not denied judgment.

Ponder: How do I approach the Lord, in prayer, in church, in worship, while God's Word is being taught, or in everyday life? Have I developed a casual attitude in approaching Him? Have I lost sight of the reality that He is not only my Father but also the holy God who is a consuming fire?

Prayer: Dear heavenly Father, I ask Your forgiveness in approaching You with a casual and irreverent attitude. I've lost sight of who You are and have become too familiar with You. I repent and will no longer see You as a "buddy" but will revere you as the holy God that You are. Thank You for being so kind and merciful and for forgiving me of my irreverence. In Jesus' name I pray, amen.

Profession: I will revere God no matter how powerfully or softly He manifests His presence.

For the LORD sees clearly

what a man does, examining

every path he takes.

—PROVERBS 5:21

10 | GOD ISN'T WATCHING

As already stated, our holy fear grows proportionally to our comprehension of God's glory. The antithesis is also true: we will diminish His greatness, even to the point of human limitations, the less we fear Him.

This world's system is like river rapids forcefully surging, even pounding upon a person's psyche in an attempt to dismiss the glory of God. The substance of this river is words, thoughts, images, videos, or any other medium that can be used to elevate mortal man at the expense of reducing the greatness of our Creator.

One who lacks holy fear easily succumbs to this force and slips into the mindset of believing that God doesn't take notice, or care about, what they do. Thoughts begin to form such as *I'm an exception*; *I'm exempt*; *I'm no different than most*; *God overlooks my motives, words, or actions*; all the way to *There's just too much going on for Him to keep track of.*

> The wicked think, "God isn't watching us! He has closed his eyes and won't even see what we do!" (Psalm 10:11)

There are several variations of this errant and dangerous mindset, but it all comes down to considering God's abilities to be inferior to what they actually are. It's no different from how we think a parent, boss, teacher, coach, or any other leader may lose track of, or not notice, our behavior. Individuals caught in this trap comfort themselves in believing there's an overabundance of details to track and couple that with lessening God's ability.

Let's take it a step further. If someone continues on this slippery path of not just lacking, but shunning, holy fear, they now are threatened with the diabolical belief that *God can't see my motives, words, or actions*. It's one thing to believe God is not watching; it is another level of irreverence to think He's *unable* to watch!

It's possible to hide our words, actions, and motives from other human beings. We can do things in secret—in the dark, even in the shadows— that others won't notice. But when we believe we can hide our thoughts or ways from God Almighty, we are self-deceived. This erroneous assumption, whether conscious or unconscious, resides in any soul devoid of holy fear. Scripture tells us,

> What sorrow awaits those who try to hide their plans from the LORD, who do their evil deeds in the dark! "The LORD can't see us," they say. "He doesn't know what's going on!" (Isaiah 29:15)

Initially you may think Isaiah refers to the wicked—unbelievers, those who would not enter a church or gather for a worship event. Yet the above is specifically written of *professing believers*. It's true, for just prior to this statement we read:

> And so the Lord says, "These people say they are mine. They honor me with their lips, but their hearts are far from me. And their worship of me is nothing but man-made rules learned by rote." (Isaiah 29:13)

Allow me to modernize this. These people profess to be in relationship with Jesus because they're saved by His grace. They verbally honor Him, attend Christian conferences, listen to worship music on Spotify—yet a part of their psyche thinks the Lord is *not able* to see or hear what they think or do. Their state of mind is worse than many who don't follow Jesus at all. They believe a lie, and even worse, they're unaware of their folly.

You may counter, "No way! This couldn't happen." Yet let's revisit the New Testament couple we brought up in the last chapter—Ananias and Sapphira (Acts 5). The backstory is important in understanding this couple's errant behavior. Their saga actually begins in chapter 4:

> Barnabas . . . a Levite of the country of Cyprus, having land, sold it, and brought the money and laid it at the apostles' feet. (Acts 4:36–37 NKJV)

During this time period, Cyprus was an island of great wealth, with an abundance of precious stones, copper and iron mines, and a great supply of lumber. It was famous for its flowers, fruit, wine, and oil. If you owned land in Cyprus, you were most likely well off.

Picture this: a wealthy Levite from Cyprus brings a very large sum of money received from the sale of his land to give openly before the entire church. What happens next?

> But there was a certain man named Ananias who, with his wife, Sapphira, sold some property. (Acts 5:1)

Notice the first word, "But." It's a conjunction that connects and continues the thought. In this case, starting the new chapter can easily detract from the continuation of the story.

This wealthy newcomer joins the church and brings a massive offering that everyone witnesses. His gift creates a reaction on the part of this couple. They immediately sell some property and . . .

> He [Ananias] brought part of the money to the apostles, claiming it was the full amount. With his wife's consent, he kept the rest. (Acts 5:2)

What initiated this response? Could it be that this couple, up to this point, had the reputation of being the biggest givers in the church? If so, did it attract the attention of the leaders and people? We must remember, giving is a gift, and just as many take notice and even applaud various gifts—such as serving, preaching, hospitality, teaching, leadership, and others—generosity is no exception; it's celebrated (2 Corinthians 9:12–13). Did this couple enjoy the respect and attention too much? Were their insecurities threatened in being outdone by the new guy? Were all the people celebrating his enormous gift, how it would help their outreaches and care for the poor, causing their focus to shift away from Ananias and his wife?

Perhaps the couple coveted the lost attention, so they responded by selling a plot of land—quite possibly their greatest asset. They reasoned, "This is far too much money to part with. But we want to *appear* to give it all. So let's only give a portion, but announce, 'It's everything we received.'" This deceptive thinking could have been strengthened by the rationalization that it would encourage others to give large gifts.

Appearance was more important than truth and, thus, led to deception. How could this couple ever think God didn't see this?

They premeditated, deliberated, and agreed upon this approach. Believing they could hide their plan from the Lord, they did their evil deed in the dark! And somewhere in their psyche they thought, *The Lord doesn't know what's going on!* (almost a direct quote from Isaiah 29:15). It cost both of them their lives; they were both buried the same day!

How did two professing believers who'd witnessed notable miracles in the previous chapters—the wind of heaven blowing and getting the attention of an entire city, thousands saved in unannounced meetings, a crippled person miraculously walking, God's power shaking a building, and more— possibly believe they could hide their motives from God Almighty?

Or how could Adam and Eve, who walked with God in the garden, possibly believe they could hide from Him after sinning (Genesis 3:8)?

How could the people of Israel say, "The LORD does not see!" (Ezekiel 9:9 NKJV)?

Or how about this shocking statement: "Son of man, have you seen what the leaders of Israel are doing with their idols in dark rooms? They are saying, 'The LORD doesn't see us'" (Ezekiel 8:12).

How often do we foolishly think we are able to hide our distant hearts from the Lord?

In short, all these scenarios have a common root that fosters this gross error: a lack of holy fear. To the degree we lack it, His abilities are diminished in our psyche, and what is most scary is that we are oblivious to our state; our discernment dulls. It's this condition that we will elaborate on in the next several chapters.

Making It Personal

Passage: Then all the churches will know that I am the one who searches out the thoughts and intentions of every person. And I will give to each of you whatever you deserve. (Revelation 2:23)

Point: God knows not only what we do but the motives and intentions behind our actions.

Ponder: Do I continually live with awareness that God knows my innermost thoughts, motives, and intentions? How can I increase my awareness of this truth?

Prayer: Dear heavenly Father, I ask that my motives and intentions would be as pure as Jesus' motives and intentions. May I filter all my thoughts, desires, words, and actions through the understanding that You continually examine my ways. May I never diminish this truth in my own perception of You. In Jesus' name I pray, amen.

Profession: I will live my life knowing God is fully aware of my intentions, thoughts, words, and actions.

Why do these people stay on their self-destructive path?

—JEREMIAH 8:5

11 | FEAR AND TREMBLING

God's awesome presence and the resulting judgment of Ananias and Sapphira brought "great fear" upon the church. Again, it should be emphasized, the word *city* is not used but rather *church*—the gathering of saints. When we examine the Greek words for *great fear*, it intensifies what's communicated.

The first word, *great*, is the Greek word *mégas*; it's defined as "the upper range of a scale . . . to a great degree, intense, terrible."[1] We get our English word *mega* from it. There's no mistaking what's communicated; in essence, it could be translated "mega fear." Keep in mind, the writers of Scripture don't overstate things.

The second word, *fear*, is the Greek word *phóbos*, a word frequently used for *holy fear* throughout the New Testament. It's defined as "fear, terror, reverence, respect, honor." Another source defines it as "profound respect and awe for deity—reverence, awe."[2] We again run into the words *awe* and *terror*, signifying a large degree of fear. Paul uses this same word when he writes,

> Therefore, my beloved, as you have always obeyed, not as in my presence only, but now much more in my absence, work out your own salvation

with *fear and trembling*; for it is God who works in you both to will and to do for His good pleasure. (Philippians 2:12–13 NKJV)

Our salvation is not worked out with *love and kindness*, rather with *fear and trembling*, which we'll examine thoroughly later. Once again, the intensity of what's being communicated is raised another notch with a new word: *trembling*. It's the Greek word *trómos*, which is defined as "a trembling from fear, terror . . . or profound reverence, respect, dread." This use is not an isolated occurrence, as the two words together are used by the apostle Paul four times in the New Testament.

Though we haven't exhausted our examination of *holy fear*, we're at a place where we can wonder how any teacher of the Word of God could limit it to "reverential worship." Just in this chapter, with the few verses we've highlighted, we've come face-to-face with some very strong vocabulary. Here's a compiled list: mega fear, awe, terror, profound respect, trembling, and dread.

These aren't just words to describe a minor aspect of our life in Christ; rather, they identify how our *salvation is worked out*—a term that describes how our efforts, in cooperation with and empowered by the Holy Spirit, bring to full maturity what Jesus freely provides for us. From this point forward, we'll say it like this: *our salvation is matured through fear and trembling*.

With this in mind, why isn't holy fear one of the forefront truths taught in our churches, small groups, and Bible schools? Could this be the cause of so many ineffective, lukewarm Christians in the Western world? And could this be the reason Scripture warns about a great "falling away" from the faith in these last days? Paul writes that the antichrist cannot be revealed until "the apostasy comes first [unless the predicted great falling away of those who have professed to be Christians has come]" (2 Thessalonians 2:3 AMPC). Could this falling away be fueled by our dumbing down holy fear? After spending forty years of prayer, study, and ministry in every state in America and sixty nations, I believe it to be so.

Let's take it a step further. One of the elementary, or foundational, teachings of the church is "eternal judgment." Carefully read these words:

Therefore, leaving the discussion of the *elementary* principles of Christ, let us go on to perfection, not laying again the *foundation* of . . . eternal judgment. (Hebrews 6:1–2 NKJV)

The fact is, all of us will give an account for the way we lived. What transpires at this judgment will last forever—it's eternal! For the believer, it is referred to as "the judgment seat of Christ."

Let's discuss the two highlighted words. First, *elementary*. What does a young child learn in elementary school? How to read, write, add, subtract, and other basic skills. In essence, we gain the building blocks needed to further our education. Can you imagine continuing on to a high school or college education without the ability to read, write, add, or subtract? Impossible!

I find many believers are unaware of the judgment they will face, or at best they are only familiar with the term but haven't investigated it thoroughly. This could be compared to merely knowing that basic elementary school skills are important but never actually learning them. A very important question to ask is, how are believers building their lives in Christ without this *elementary* truth?

Let's consider the other highlighted word, *foundation*. Can you imagine erecting a building without a foundation? If the weather is calm, the building can rise high and remain standing. But when a strong storm arrives, down comes the building! This could represent a departure from the faith. The Barna Group reported that more than forty million Americans departed from the faith from the years 2000 to 2020![3] Half now profess to be non-Christians—atheists and agnostics. Could our lack of *foundational* teaching contribute to this catastrophic statistic?

Let's take a brief look at what's attached to our judgment:

We are confident, yes, well pleased rather to be absent from the body and to be present with the Lord. (2 Corinthians 5:8 NKJV)

Immediately, we know Paul is speaking only to believers. When an unbeliever is absent from the body they are not in God's presence.

Therefore we make it our aim, whether present or absent, to be well *pleasing* to Him. (2 Corinthians 5:9 NKJV)

When our sons were in their teenage years, Lisa and I looked for opportunities to train them in godliness. One important aspect of their training was to protect them from developing an attitude of entitlement. One evening I said to them, "Guys, you cannot do one thing to make your mother and me love you any more or less than we already do."

Our unconditional love for them registered. But a few moments later I followed this statement with, "But, you are responsible for how *pleased* we are with you." It was an eye-opening moment for them.

Here's the truth. We cannot do anything to make God love us more or less, but we are responsible for how pleased He is with us. This is why Paul says it's his goal to be "well pleasing." Why?

For we [believers] must all appear before the judgment seat of Christ, that each one may receive the things done in the body, according to what he has done, whether good or bad. Knowing, therefore, *the terror of the Lord*, we persuade men. (2 Corinthians 5:10–11 NKJV)

At this judgment seat we will not be judged for our repented sins—they have already been eradicated by the blood of Jesus. God "has removed our sins as far from us as the east is from the west" (Psalm 103:12). Again, He says, "I will forgive their wickedness, and I will never again remember their sins" (Hebrews 8:12).

So what will our judgment entail? We'll be examined regarding how we lived as believers, and both *good* and *bad* will be examined.

What's important to our current discussion is that Paul attaches "the *terror* of the Lord" with the believer's judgment. As mentioned before, the Greek word for *terror* is *phóbos*, the very word used to describe the church's reaction to Ananias and Sapphira's judgment. This brings us to an important question: could the incident of this couple be a sneak preview of the believer's judgment? We'll explore this possibility in the next couple of chapters.

======================= **Making It Personal** =======================

Passage: That you may walk (live and conduct yourselves) in a manner worthy of the Lord, *fully pleasing* to Him and *desiring to please Him* in all things, bearing fruit in every good work. (Colossians 1:10 AMPC)

Point: You cannot do anything to make God love you more or less than He already does. But you are responsible for how pleased He is with you.

Ponder: Is my life pleasing to God? How do I know what does and doesn't please Him?

Prayer: Dear heavenly Father, I ask that You reveal to me through Your Word and by Your Spirit what is pleasing and displeasing to You. Give me a heart and mind that would pursue Your pleasure and delight more than anything else. In doing so may I come to know Your heart and live in a way that honors You. May what I ask prepare me to one day face the believer's judgment and receive the eternal rewards You desire to give me. In Jesus' name I pray, amen.

Profession: Pleasing God is my first priority in life. He is working in me both to will and to do His good pleasure.

The remarkable thing about God is that when you fear God, you fear nothing else, whereas if you do not fear God, you fear everything else.

—OSWALD CHAMBERS

12 | CONTAGIOUS HYPOCRISY

It's important to clarify an important point regarding the couple whose lives ended in the book of Acts. The issue wasn't Ananias and Sapphira's actions; they simply gave an offering at their church service. It is godly, holy, and beautiful to give a financial gift to the work of God. The sin was their motive—the desire to be viewed in a certain light.

This brings up an important question: will only our words and works be examined at the judgment seat, or will our thoughts and motives be included?

Let's start by reading a warning Jesus spoke to His disciples:

In the meantime, when an innumerable multitude of people had gathered together, so that they trampled one another, He began to say to His disciples first of all, "Beware of the leaven of the Pharisees, which is *hypocrisy*. For there is nothing covered that will not be revealed, nor hidden that will not be known." (Luke 12:1–2 NKJV)

So much is laid out in these two verses. Imagine you're a minister of the gospel and such a large crowd gathers to hear you that it's recorded as "innumerable." This is most preachers' dream! Yet what does Jesus do? He doesn't whisper to His team, "Hey guys, this is what I'm here for. Step aside while I do My thing!" No. Instead, He does three things:

First, He seizes the opportunity to impart to them an illustrated message of *how not to be controlled by the moment*. He warns these future leaders, both by example and teaching, about *hypocrisy*. It's the Greek word *hupókrisis* and is defined as "to give an impression of having certain purposes or motivations, while in reality having quite different ones."[1]

The Pharisees were experts in hypocrisy—doing things for show and pretense. Jesus warns not to fall into this trap by remaining pure in motive. In essence, He is communicating, don't let popularity or mankind's approval drive you, but be led by the Spirit, staying firm in truth both in what you teach and how you live.

Second, Jesus points out how quickly hypocrisy can spread. He compares it to leaven, which is yeast that spreads throughout the dough and causes the entire batch to rise. Jesus' illustration conveys that hypocrisy is contagious, but unlike yeast, it's very detrimental to our well-being.

Third, He emphatically states that hypocrisy cannot stay hidden. It's certain that the intent behind one's words or actions will eventually be exposed. His next statement reveals what protects from impure motives:

> My friends, do not be afraid of those who kill the body, and after that have no more that they can do. But I will show you whom you should fear: Fear Him who, after He has killed, has power to cast into hell; yes, I say to you, fear Him! (Luke 12:4–5 NKJV)

Once again, Jesus uses strong language for *fear*. Its *phobéō*, which is akin to *phóbos*, our highlighted word in the previous chapter. *Phobéō* is defined as "to put in fear, terrify, frighten." Jesus links being "cast into hell" with ignoring holy fear. This is a terrifying thought that shouldn't be taken lightly. Again, we see holy fear's importance, and it's once again confirmed to be more than reverential worship.

Jesus tells us to fear God, not people. Simply put, *the fear of God frees us from the fear of man*, and *the fear of man enslaves us by removing our ability to fear God*. Make no mistake, when we fear people, our motives will be affected. Think of the "fear of man" in a similar fashion to the "fear of God." It's not necessarily running from people; rather, it gravitates toward pleasing those before us, with the underlying motive of personal satisfaction, protection, or gain. The fear of man ensnares us in the yeast of hypocrisy. It leads to living for man's approval.

Again, Ananias and Sapphira's actions seemed beyond reproach; however, their motivation propelled them to project a certain image to their community, and this is what brought them down. People can perform actions and speak words that are godly, but without holy fear they commit sin by their intentions.

When I was serving in my local church in the 1980s, I was terribly bound to the fear of man. I didn't realize it until the Holy Spirit exposed my motivation. At the time I had a high-profile position in our megachurch. I was consistently kind to those I interacted with and was always quick to give a compliment, even if it wasn't true. I hated confrontation and avoided it like a plague. Reports began to circle back to me that I was one of the most loving men in the church. It brought happiness and satisfaction to me.

One day in prayer I heard the Lord say, "Son, people say you are a loving and kind man." I distinctly recall the way He spoke it to my heart; I didn't sense His tone to be affirming.

So, I cautiously said, "Yes, they do say that."

He responded, "Do you know why you speak nice and complimentary things to people even if it isn't true?"

"Why?"

"Because you fear their rejection. So, who is the focus of your love—you or them? If you really loved people, you would speak truth and not lie, even at the expense of being rejected." I was stunned. Everyone else pegged me as a loving man, but the underlying truth was quite different.

In the same manner, the members of the early church most likely considered Ananias and Sapphira to be godly, especially as he was bringing a substantial gift to their pastor before the assembly. But their true motives were exposed. In the same way, my motives were self-promoting, self-protecting, and self-rewarding. The real story of my behavior was that of a hypocrite.

It's easy to do godly, beneficial works before a watching world, all the while concealing a self-seeking motive. We can move a crowd with a great gospel message but inwardly be motivated by selfish ambition (Philippians 1:15–16). We can give huge gifts to the poor but do so void of love (1 Corinthians 13:3). We can lead people in worship but have a hidden intent to be known or famous. We can be kind in our interactions but inwardly scrutinize and criticize others. We can affirm our sorrow over a pastor who's been asked to resign for an immoral failure but inwardly rejoice that he got what he deserved. We can appear humble and proclaim, "All the glory goes to Jesus," while inwardly we love the affirmation and praise. The list is endless.

Here is the raw truth: First, not one motive or intention can be hidden from God, and second, it will eventually be revealed. The important question is: Is it hidden from us? The fear of the Lord keeps us in touch with our heart motives, which is critically important, for the lack thereof leaves us vulnerable to the deception of hypocrisy.

The church people were all shocked by Ananias's judgment, but they were no more shocked than Ananias himself, and then later, Sapphira. This couple's lack of holy fear blinded them to the wickedness of their own motives. Again, we must ask, is their story a preview of the judgment seat of Christ? We will see in the next chapter.

Making It Personal

Passage: For the word of God is living and powerful, and sharper than any two-edged sword . . . and is a discerner of the thoughts and intents of the heart. (Hebrews 4:12 NKJV)

Point: The fear of the Lord keeps us in touch with our heart motives, which is critically important, for the lack thereof leaves us vulnerable to the deception of hypocrisy.

Ponder: How do I gravitate toward pleasing others with the underlying motive of personal satisfaction, protection, or gain? Is this something I default to when under pressure? In what areas has it caused me to compromise my integrity?

Prayer: Dear heavenly Father, I ask You to forgive me for seeking to please others for my benefit. Holy Spirit, I ask You to expose all areas of my life where I easily give in to this pressure. I repent of making people my source of joy and happiness rather than making Jesus my source. I ask you to fill my heart with holy fear so that I will consistently love others in truth and so that I will not succumb to hypocrisy. In Jesus' name I pray, amen.

Profession: I will love those I interact with by speaking truth and seeking their benefit over my own.

For we must all appear and be revealed as we are before the judgment seat of Christ.

—2 CORINTHIANS 5:10 AMPC

13 | THREE IMAGES

Look closely at the phrase "revealed as we are" in the verse on the opposite page. Every human being has three images of themselves: a *perceived* image, a *projected* image, and an *actual* image.

Our *perceived* image is how others see us. Our *projected* image is the way we desire others to see us. Our *actual* image is who we really are, and while it can be hidden or unnoticed by others, it's fully visible to God. It's how we'll be revealed before all at the judgment seat.

Consider Jesus—He was misunderstood, falsely accused, identified as a drunkard and glutton, labeled as a heretic, and even accused of being demon-inspired. He was rejected by religious leaders and others. His *perceived* image was unfavorable in the eyes of many, especially the notables.

Jesus' stepbrothers—skeptics at the time—pressured Him to live out of a *projected* image: "Go where your followers can see your miracles!" they scoffed. "You can't become famous if you hide like this! . . . Show yourself to the world!" (John 7:3–4). They were controlled by others' perceptions and attempted to bring Jesus under the same slavery—the fear of man.

Yet Jesus' *actual* image is quite different from the one many *perceived*, for "He is the visible image of the invisible God" (Colossians 1:15). While many were rejecting Him, God Almighty audibly affirmed, "This is my dearly loved Son, who brings me great joy" (Matthew 3:17). Jesus' *perceived* image is not what endured, rather His *actual* image.

While on earth, He shunned self-promotion and any efforts to build His own reputation. When healing someone in need He often said, "'Don't tell anyone about this'" (Matthew 9:30). He avoided popularity, notoriety, and the accolades and approval of men.[1] When people wanted to promote Him to be king, He pulled away. There was no facade, nor were there any false illusions or deceit in Him. He delighted in the fear of the Lord, which kept His focus on the Father.

We should also be the express image of Jesus. Freedom is found in living according to the truth in our inward parts, while avoiding self-promotion or self-preservation. We discover the origin of self-focused behavior in Adam and Eve. We read the moment they fell, ". . . their eyes were opened, and they suddenly felt shame" (Genesis 3:7). Their focus shifted off of God to themselves, and now they sought to alleviate their newly discovered short-comings. The first couple tried to *cover* their nakedness. With us it may manifest differently, but the root problem is still the same. If I'm self-focused, then I'll seek to project an image that will *cover* my known inadequacies. Jesus gave His life to free us from this slavery. Paul writes: "For we dare not class ourselves or compare ourselves with those who commend themselves. But they, measuring themselves by themselves, and comparing themselves among themselves, are not wise" (2 Corinthians 10:12 NKJV).

If we succumb to the pressure of comparison, we highlight our short-comings and in turn will self-promote or self-protect, and it all begins in our motives and intentions. In today's world our *perceived* image carries greater weight than our *actual* image. Simply put, our reputation is what we will protect. Our efforts now focus on appearances, status, titles, popularity, acceptance, reputation, and so forth, for they *cover* our shortcomings.

This is not what will be revealed and examined at the judgment; rather it will be our *actual* image, which centers around our motives and intentions.

So don't make judgments about anyone ahead of time—before the Lord returns. For he will bring our *darkest secrets* to light and will reveal our *private motives*. Then God will give to each one whatever *praise* is due. (1 Corinthians 4:5)

Many discount this Scripture thinking it applies to the unbeliever's judgment. Not so, for no unbeliever will receive praise at their judgment. This can only speak of believers.

When you hear of your "darkest secrets" and "private motives" being revealed before the entire assembly of heaven, it likely makes you fear in a healthy way. This could be one reason Paul refers to believer's judgment as "the terror of the Lord." Our awareness of its reality creates a holy fear, which in turn keeps us in check and enables us live from our *actual* image. However, the antithesis also holds true: the more we lack the fear of the Lord, the more we will lean on our *projected* image.

This was Ananias and Sapphira's deadly trap. They were more interested in how they were *perceived* by those they saw as their rivals, friends, church members, and leaders.

To make their story more relatable, let's imagine the journey that led to their downfall as if it happened in modern times. The church hadn't existed more than a few months. The apostles and church members were all watching to see who would emerge as leaders in different areas.

For this couple, it was a happy day when they received Jesus and were forgiven of their sins. They were overwhelmed by the love of God and the community of fellow believers.

However, their focus would eventually shift. Interestingly enough, it most likely began by God working through them—maybe an offering, an exhortation, singing on the worship team—the possibilities are endless. They enjoyed feeling the gratification that comes from their service being recognized. The endorphins surged and brought exhilarating feelings of happiness and satisfaction.

Their recognition grew. However, to maintain their newly formed reputation, they needed to *cover* some questionable behavior with seemingly harmless words and actions. Perhaps they found themselves in an intense domestic disagreement followed by an extended fight. Their anger and arguments grew ugly and lingered, but when the time came to gather with believers, they drastically altered their behavior to *cover* their shortcoming. The couple didn't want their peers to see their disagreements and strife, which would threaten their *perceived* image, so they *projected* a loving and caring attitude toward each other.

They posted pictures and videos on Instagram and TikTok of hugging, smiling, and enjoying fun activities together. The captions read something like "living the dream" or "relationship goals" or "I love doing life with her [or him]!" There were numerous other posts depicting their successful life (which was struggling), growing business (which was on a downturn), beautiful children (whose behavior was defiant, entitled, and selfish), and other successes. It seemed to work because the number of their social media followers was rapidly increasing.

Ananias and Sapphira were in a pattern of keeping their *projected* image strong. It all seemed harmless, yet their godly fear was gradually diminishing with every act of hypocrisy. They were no longer convicted in their duplicity. All seemed well, and they enjoyed a good reputation, part of which was being the most generous givers in the church.

The day came when Barnabas brought his offering before the church. The attention of their peers suddenly shifted. They were outdone, and their *perceived* image was threatened. Sadly, by this time, the emphasis on their self-made image had already been well-developed. The rest is history.

It all seemed harmless and inspiring to others, but it led them down a dangerous and destructive path. Did the Holy Spirit give us this couple's fate in Scripture to warn us and provide a glimpse of how serious the judgment seat will be? Paul writes:

> The sins of some men are conspicuous (openly evident to all eyes), going before them to the judgment [seat] *and* proclaiming their sentence in advance; but the sins of others appear later [following the offender to the bar of judgment and coming into view there]. (1 Timothy 5:24 AMPC)

Ananias and Sapphira's sin was made openly evident to all on that memorable day. Their judgment was proclaimed in advance. However, what should be more alarming is that the sins of most will be made evident later. Please remember, God's verdict addressed their secret motive, not their action.

Here is the good news: we can repent of our dark motives, and God will not only forgive, but if we cry out to Him for holy fear and renew our mind through Scripture, we can be blessed with pure motives.

Making It Personal

Passage: "For all that is secret will eventually be brought into the open, and everything that is concealed will be brought to light and made known to all." (Luke 8:17)

Point: Every human being has three images: a *perceived* image, a *projected* image, and an *actual* image.

Ponder: What image do I gravitate toward? Do I live from a place of truth, or do I lie or make deceptive statements to protect my reputation? Am I honest and forthright with those I'm in relationship with?

Prayer: I repent of putting more emphasis on my projected and perceived image rather than my actual image. I've compromised integrity and ask Your forgiveness. Purify my motives and intentions. May my focus center on Jesus and others, not myself.

Profession: I will allow the double-edged sword of God's Word to expose the thoughts and intentions of my heart.

The fear of death and judgment goes out of us as the true fear of God comes in, and that fear has no torment but is rather a light and easy yoke for the soul, one which rests us instead of exhausting us.

—A. W. TOZER AND HARRY VERPLOEGH

14 | ETERNAL DECISIONS

Compared to eternity, this present life is a vapor. But even more accurate, this life is nothing, for simple mathematics states that any finite number divided by infinity is zero. Therefore, ninety or so years compared to eternity is equal to nothing. In light of this startling reality, it's wise to prepare for the everlasting.

The decisions Jesus makes over each of us at the judgment seat are *eternal* (Hebrews 6:1–2). Simply put, there will never be any changes, revisions, or alterations made to His pronouncements. So, in essence, what we do with the cross determines *where* we will spend eternity; however, the *way* we live as believers determines *how* we will live in the forever.

Too many have the concept of heaven consisting of nothing more than a disembodied, nonphysical experience with love, peace, and no suffering accompanying it. They anticipate saints being ethereal beings floating on clouds, playing harps, and eating grapes. Still others view heaven as one dull, nonstop worship service. With these views it is hard to get excited about this tedious eternal existence.

But these are myths, found nowhere in Scripture. The best of this life is but a shadow of the eternal. There will be communities to plan, cities to build, nations to oversee, galaxies to explore and develop, and infinitely more that aligns with how we were created to live. There are positions of responsibility to be filled for the Lord's eternal city. So, view the judgment seat as the interview and evaluation that determine your everlasting position in His capital city of the new heaven and the new earth.

With this in mind, let's get back to discussing how the here and now is examined at the judgment:

> For we must all appear and be revealed as we are before the judgment seat of Christ, so that each one may receive [his pay] according to what he has done in the body, whether good or evil [considering what his purpose and motive have been, and what he has achieved, been busy with, and given himself and his attention to accomplishing]. (2 Corinthians 5:10 AMPC)

As believers, our sins, which would have condemned us to hell, are eradicated by the blood of Jesus and are forever forgotten (Hebrews 8:12). Yet there is still evil or bad behavior that we will have to give an account for at the believer's judgment. This should get our attention.

The word *evil* is the Greek word *kakós* and is defined as "pertaining to being bad, with the implication of harmful and damaging" and to "recede, retire, retreat in battle." This word implies a damaging effect, one that can be caused not only by what we do but also by retreating or retiring, or more simply stated, by what we *don't* do. Therefore, it encompasses not only what we did but also missed opportunities. Holy fear keeps us alert to kingdom responsibilities, as well as any adverse motives or behaviors damaging the lives of those God loves.

Often Scripture refers to us as "builders." You could view it as being subcontractors erecting God's custom home that He will dwell in forever. His home has a name—*Zion* (Psalm 132:13–14)—and its material consists of living stones—all His saints (1 Peter 2:5), with Jesus being the chief cornerstone (Isaiah 28:16).

Paul clearly identifies our assignments: "We are His workmanship, created in Christ Jesus for good works, which God prepared beforehand that we *should* walk in them" (Ephesians 2:10 NKJV). Notice Paul writes we *should*, not *would*, fulfill these tasks. If we retreat from our assignments by choosing to live in a way that is motivated by temporary selfish gain, this would be considered one of the "evil" behaviors.

Paul also writes, "Whoever is building on this foundation must be very careful" (1 Corinthians 3:10). It's clear that how we build is of the essence. Are we building with His eternal Word or are we listening to the spirit of this age? Are we building by His Spirit or are we catering to our self-seeking desires? Paul continues:

> Anyone who builds on that foundation may use a variety of materials—gold, silver, jewels, wood, hay, or straw. But on the judgment day, fire will reveal what kind of work each builder has done. The fire will show if a person's work has any value. (1 Corinthians 3:12–13)

There is a variety of ways we can choose to spend our God-given time. If we live to build for self-gain—the temporary—it's considered combustible material. If we live selflessly to build His eternal kingdom, it's viewed as material that isn't destroyed but purified. The fire that examines our lives will be the Word of God—in other words, how did our motives, words, and behavior line up with it?

Paul goes on to say, "If the work survives, that builder will receive a reward" (v. 14). If our behavior and labor stem from obedience to His Word and will for our lives, our achievements will last forever. There are two things to note: First, our achievements will include how we influenced others' lives, along with how we used our God-given talents to build His kingdom. Second, our eternal reward will determine our eternal position in His kingdom.

Paul's next words are riveting:

> But if the work is burned up, the builder will suffer *great* loss. The builder will be *saved*, but like someone barely escaping through a wall of flames. (1 Corinthians 3:15)

There is so much to unpack in this verse. First, notice the builder is *saved*. This is not about an unbeliever who is condemned to the lake of fire forever, but rather one who will eternally reside in God's kingdom.

Second, the loss is great. The Greek word used here can imply punishment or loss. Most scholars don't believe it's punishment, nor do I. However, the word does suggest a sense of profound loss. Keep in mind this intense loss will not only be felt at the judgment but will also affect how we live forever.

Third, the comparison given is like one barely escaping through a wall of flames. Let's try to modernize this. Westerners often prepare for retirement. (I personally don't subscribe to this mentality, as retirement speaks of retreating from an assignment—a definition of "evil" [*kakós*]. However, since it is relatable, I'll use retirement for illustration purposes.)

Imagine on the day someone retires, the bank goes belly-up. All of the retiree's savings are lost, and all he has are the few dollars in his wallet. That same day Social Security and all the companies holding his IRAs go bankrupt. Not only this, but the retiree's home burns to the ground, and he escapes with just the shirt on his back. He's lost everything. This is a scenario that would be considered a disaster. Yet this is the description Paul uses to describe how some believers will enter eternity. And it's not for a period of twenty-five years (the average length of retirement); it is for all eternity.

Again, Paul says the believer is saved, yet everything is burned up and forever lost. Remember, it's an eternal judgment (decision). Please don't misunderstand—to be saved is nothing insignificant; it is infinitely better than being lost in the lake of fire for all eternity. We all will rejoice beyond comprehension—but there will be a sense of what could have been.

No wonder Paul follows this with the words, "Knowing, therefore, the *terror of the Lord*, we persuade men" (2 Corinthians 5:11 NKJV). Please hear my heart—it is my hope that this holy fear Paul identifies will persuade you to not waste your time on things that do not profit or to spend it focused on your projected and perceived image. It's my hope that your gift of time is dedicated in obedience to His Word and Spirit.

Making It Personal

Passage: For we must all appear before the judgment seat of Christ, that each one may receive the things done in the body, according to what he has done, whether good or bad. Knowing, therefore, the terror of the Lord, we persuade men. (2 Corinthians 5:10–11 NKJV)

Point: What we do with the cross determines *where* we'll spend eternity; however, the way we live as a believer determines *how* we'll live in the forever.

Ponder: Do I focus each day on building for the eternal—building others' lives with truth and love—or do I give my strength, energy, and time to building for myself?

Prayer: Dear heavenly Father, forgive me for giving my focused attention, energy, strength, and time to building for the temporal. I ask that You show me how to build for Jesus' kingdom on a daily basis. Please empower me to impact people's lives for the eternal. Thank You in Jesus' name, amen.

Profession: I will look for and engage in eternal opportunities, not merely the ones that perish with this life.

Irresistible Holiness

WEEK 3

The carnal person fears man, not God. The strong Christian fears God, not man. The weak Christian fears man too much, and God too little.

—JOHN FLAVEL

15 | THE FEAR OF MAN

True holiness is to be completely God's. A primary definition of holiness is "separation unto God."[1] Its breadth of meaning is so vast that volumes could be written on it. Here we will cover the highlights, as godly fear is an integral aspect of holiness. But before we embark, it is important to clearly state up front: authentic holiness isn't bondage; it's true freedom.

It's quite possible Ananias and Sapphira's judgment is a prelude to what every human being will one day face—judgment. The lingering question is, is this couple an example of those who suffer "great loss" in heaven, or did they find themselves in Hades?

The scripture often used to explain this couple's eternal damnation is found earlier in the Gospels in Jesus' words: "He who blasphemes against the Holy Spirit never has forgiveness" (Mark 3:29 NKJV). The errancy of this thought is exposed by the definition of *blaspheme*, which means "to speak against someone in such a way as to harm or injure his or her reputation."[2] This couple *lied* to the Holy Spirit, but by definition, they didn't *blaspheme*. This keeps their fate inconclusive. In either case, none of us should ever envy their outcome.

So, do we have an example in Scripture of someone we know is in heaven but will suffer certain loss at the judgment seat? I believe so. Allow me to set it up with Paul's words:

> Does this sound as if I am trying to win human approval? No indeed! What I want is God's approval! Am I trying to be popular with people? If I were still trying to do so, I would not be a servant of Christ. (Galatians 1:10 GNT)

What a strong statement. We forfeit the privilege to be a servant of Christ if we succumb to the pull of seeking popularity. In doing so, we will project whatever image is necessary for a favorable perception. Paul would have nothing to do with this, and we should be no different.

Paul walked in a high level of holy fear; remember, he is the one who scribed, "Work out your own salvation with fear and trembling" (Philippians 2:12 NKJV). He stayed focused on his *actual* image—the one that will be revealed at the judgment—not his *projected* image. This kept him in the place of true holiness and obedience to Christ, even when met with the disappointment, disapproval, or rejection of others.

We should keep this truth before us at all times: *You will serve whom you fear!* If you fear God, you'll obey God. If you fear man, you'll ultimately obey man's desires. Often we worry more about offending the person before us than the One we don't physically see, especially if we desire a person's love or friendship. For this reason, we are told, "Fearing people is a dangerous trap" (Proverbs 29:25)—a trap Ananias and Sapphira certainly fell into.

I can only imagine that an encounter with fellow leaders fueled Paul's fire, compelling him to write these confrontational words later in this same letter:

> When Peter came to Antioch, I had a face-to-face confrontation with him because he was clearly out of line. Here's the situation. Earlier, before certain persons had come from James, Peter regularly ate with the non-Jews. But when that conservative group came from Jerusalem, he cautiously pulled back and put as much distance as he could manage between

himself and his non-Jewish friends. That's how fearful he was of the con-servative Jewish clique that's been pushing the old system of circumcision. Unfortunately, the rest of the Jews in the Antioch church joined in that hypocrisy so that even Barnabas was swept along in the charade.

But when I saw that they were not maintaining a steady, straight course according to the Message, I spoke up to Peter in front of them all: "If you, a Jew, live like a non-Jew when you're not being observed by the watchdogs from Jerusalem, what right do you have to require non-Jews to conform to Jewish customs just to make a favorable impression on your old Jerusalem buddies?" (Galatians 2:11–14 MSG)

Peter, Barnabas, and the other Jewish believers were afraid of disapproval from those they respected. Their desire for acceptance led to hypocritical behavior—first from Peter and then from the others. Their *projected* image took precedence over integrity, thus leading to behavior that wasn't holy. Another version of Proverbs 29:25 tells us, "It is dangerous to be concerned with what others think of you" (GNT).

Paul, who maintained his integrity, rebuked Peter to his face, along with Barnabas and the others who gave in to peer pressure. Paul was quick to point out that if the conservative Jewish leaders were absent, Peter and com-pany lived according to truth, their *actual* image. They were empowered to be true representatives of Jesus Christ—to accept, love, and fellowship with the new Gentile believers. But once the dynamic changed, Peter and friends switched over to *project* an image to gratify their contemporaries. The con-sequences of their behavior weren't edifying but damaging.

Peter is a saint; he's in heaven. However, this is an example of the evil or damaging motives, words, and actions that will be examined at the judg-ment seat. If we live with the consistent goal of pleasing Jesus, we will not slip over to being controlled by how others *perceive* us; instead, we'll live in truth. This is an important aspect of true holiness. Carefully read this:

God's word is alive and working and is sharper than a double-edged sword. It cuts all the way into us, where the soul and the spirit are joined, to the center of our joints and bones. And it judges the thoughts and feelings in our hearts. Nothing in all the world can be hidden from God. Everything is clear and lies open before him, and to him we must explain the way we have lived. (Hebrews 4:12–13 NCV)

Did you take in these words? If you skimmed over them because of familiarity, reread them slowly and ponder each statement.

Notice the Word of God pierces deep into our innermost thoughts and desires. It exposes us for who we really are, not who we project ourselves to be. If listened to and obeyed, God's Word protects us from self-deception— such as the thought, *The Lord doesn't see us*, which causes ungodly or unholy behavior.

Carefully heeding the Word of God keeps the fear of the Lord active in our hearts. It keeps us fully aware of the fact that "nothing in all creation is hidden from God. Everything is naked and exposed before his eyes" (Hebrews 4:13). Now we have a better understanding of why the Holy Spirit counsels us:

> My son [or daughter], if you receive my words, and treasure my commands within you, so that you incline your ear to wisdom, and apply your heart to understanding; yes, if you cry out for discernment, and lift up your voice for understanding, if you seek her as silver, and search for her as for hidden treasures; then you will understand the fear of the LORD. (Proverbs 2:1–5 NKJV)

It is most wise to pursue His Word in our inward parts—the place that governs our motives and intentions. When we view God's Word as the greatest treasure to be found and obey what's revealed, we enter into the *safety zone*. When we earnestly seek to know His ways as if there were no superior reward, then we know and understand the fear of the Lord and avoid the deception of projecting a false image. We are now empowered to live by integrity and truth and have securely planted our feet on the highway (pathway) of holiness.

Making It Personal

Passage: Make the Lord of Heaven's Armies holy in your life. He is the one you should fear. He is the one who should make you tremble. He will keep you safe. (Isaiah 8:13–14)

Point: You will serve whom you fear. If you fear God, you'll obey God. If you fear man, you'll ultimately obey man's desires. If you seek to obey others' desires, you can no longer be a true servant of Jesus Christ.

Ponder: Why do I try harder not to offend the person before me than the One I don't physically see? Why do I desire love, acceptance, and friendship from people more than from God? How can I change this?

Prayer: Dear heavenly Father, I ask You to forgive me for the times I've sought the approval of others rather than Your approval. Jesus, I repent of seeking popularity with people over Your approval. I choose to be holy, set apart for You. From this moment forward, You are the one I ultimately seek to please. In Jesus' name, amen.

Profession: I am a servant of Christ. I seek His approval over the approval of others.

Wherever the fear of God rules in the heart, it will appear both in works of charity and piety, and neither will excuse us from the other.

—MATTHEW HENRY

16 | ENTITLEMENT

The book of Galatians was written around AD 49, so we can conclude Paul's correction of Peter and the other Jewish leaders occurred before this time. More than a decade later, approximately AD 63, Peter wrote his first epistle. I'm sure the confrontation, which was made known to the entire Galatian church, was still vivid in his memory when he scribed these words:

> Don't slip back into your old ways of living to satisfy your own desires. You didn't know any better then . . . And remember that the heavenly Father to whom you pray has no favorites. He will judge or reward you according to what you do. So you must live in *reverent fear* of him during your time here as "temporary residents." (1 Peter 1:14, 17)

It's obvious Peter is writing to believers—those who have denied themselves, are crucified to the world, and are fully dedicated to following Jesus. Any manner of conversion outside of this foundation is not authentic (Matthew 16:24; Mark 8:34; Luke 9:23; Galatians 6:14). Once regeneration occurs, a divine nature is formed within us. Yielding to this nature frees us from the dictates of our senses, and we are empowered to do so by His Spirit and God's revealed Word (2 Peter 1:4).

The apostle warns us not to revert back to living according to our own desires that formerly controlled us. One of the strongest cravings we must deny and crucify is *self-preservation*. It's the core motivation behind projecting ourselves to be perceived favorably by others—in other words, the fear of man. This propelled not only Peter's detrimental behavior but also that of Ananias, Sapphira, Barnabas, and others.

Peter warns that we will be unfavorably judged, either in this life or the next, if we yield to these cravings. Conversely, we'll be rewarded for closely adhering to God's desires. In the midst of these instructions, he gives a stern warning: *God has no favorites*. Let's consider what could have been behind this comment.

This apostle was given a powerful ministry by Jesus. He was one of the top leaders of the early church, yet years prior while in Antioch, he and his fellow Jewish leaders fell into this self-serving trap. Perhaps Paul's eye-opening confrontation prompted an honest assessment of his own motives and actions. In essence, Peter had to face off with the "why" behind his hypocrisy.

Perhaps in this face-off, he pondered the errant behavior of other biblical leaders, such as King Saul and King David. Saul disobeyed a clear directive from heaven in order to earn favor with his military—the fear of man. David committed adultery, then murdered the woman's husband to save his reputation—the fear of man. Both leaders were confronted, and both brought forms of judgment on themselves. For Saul, he lost his kingdom. For David, the sword would never leave his household. Falling into the trap of thinking they were favored of God, both compromised healthy personal boundaries and consequently strayed into ungodly or disobedient behavior.

Peter was aware of how easily this can occur. He warned us to avoid "entitled" thoughts, which we think exempt us from judgment, such as: "I work diligently for God," or "I've given much to build His kingdom," or "I've spent years interceding and praying," or "I've accomplished much as a church leader." Let's face it, these deceptive reasonings are endless, but they all boil down to, *I've been given a free pass*. This mentality abandons the treasure of holy fear.

Peter began to more fully comprehend the weight of Jesus' statement when He said, "When you obey me you should say, 'We are unworthy servants who have simply done our duty'" (Luke 17:10). The Greek word for "unworthy" is defined as "not deserving special praise, not worthy of particular commendation."[1] No matter how diligently we've served God, we should never fall into an entitled attitude. It's the deceptive psyche that easily entraps all of us, especially leaders.

In his letters, Peter's now writing with experience and revelation. He knows the antidote to the fear of man is to live in reverent fear. Again, it speaks of profound respect and awe. He is giving us the key that positions us to be rewarded by God, rather than to be judged unfavorably.

In this light, if we examine Jesus' teaching of "the narrow gate and difficult path," a startling reality is made clear that many miss.

"Enter by the narrow gate; for wide *is* the gate and broad *is* the way that leads to destruction, and there are many who go in by it. Because narrow is the gate and difficult is *the way* (*path*) which leads to life, and there are few who find it." (Matthew 7:13–14 NKJV)

Jesus speaks of the narrow gate, which most believe is the entrance to eternal life through the lordship of Jesus. I agree.

However, I have discovered that "the way" (path or road) is thought by many to be the unbeliever's path that leads to destruction. But if you look closely, you will see He likely isn't speaking of the path *before* finding the gate but the path *after* walking through it. Leon Morris writes, "We enter the gate right at the beginning (i.e., we commit ourselves to following Christ), after which we pursue the path before us."[2] Jesus is speaking of our life in Him after we are saved. He declares it's difficult (or narrow).

The grace that is so popular in our Western church has broadened that path. It proclaims, "All our sins, past, present, and future, are forgiven." This is true in proper context, but we are told this in such a way as to think we can live the broad life, not much different from a lost world, and still be in fellowship with God. This isn't true, for the rest of the words from Peter's writings above state:

> Don't slip back into your old ways of living to satisfy your own desires. You didn't know any better then. But now you *must be* holy in everything you do, just as God who chose you is holy. For the Scriptures say, "You must be holy because I am holy." (1 Peter 1:14–16)

Holiness is not a "should be" recommendation; rather it is a "must be" command. We are wise to heed the former, but we are fools to take lightly the commands of God. Furthermore, Peter is not talking about our position in Christ but our actions. We must live in *phóbos* (holy fear) to attain this lifestyle. God has given us two great forces to help us stay clear of the ditches that would entrap us on either side of the narrow road. The first ditch is *legalism*, and the second one is *lawlessness*.

Many in the church were in the *legalism* ditch years ago. In those days holiness centered around man-made lifestyle requirements that were unscriptural. They preached a false gospel of salvation by works. It was terrible bondage and led many to resentment and some even leaving the faith. A major revelation delivered us from this horrible trench: *God is a good God*. Our heavenly Father's *love* became real and pulled many out of this ditch of legalism.

But we did what human beings often do—we determined to get so far from the legalistic trench that we strayed to the opposite side and fell into the *lawlessness* ditch. This ditch ensnares us into believing we are saved by an unscriptural grace that permits us to live no differently than the rest of the world—we can now live according to the desires that stem from our senses rather than a crucified life that draws from the power of Christ within. This is a lie that prevents many from experiencing the presence, blessing, and power of God.

Holiness is not bondage; rather, it is the true liberty that opens the way to enjoy both God and this life. We are called to live a life worthy of the

One who rescued us. It is by the fear of the Lord that we walk in it, and we'll elaborate on this truth in our next few chapters.

Making It Personal

Passage: And a great road will go through that once deserted land. It will be named the Highway of Holiness. Evil-minded people will never travel on it. It will be only for those who walk in God's ways; fools will never walk there. (Isaiah 35:8)

Point: The love of God protects us from the ditch of legalism. Conversely, the fear of the Lord protects us from the ditch of lawlessness. Holy fear empowers me to stay on the highway of true holiness.

Ponder: In what ways do I ignore holy fear and tolerate ungodly behavior in my life? How has my service in the kingdom given me permission to ignore the command to be holy as God is holy? And what sense of entitlement has caused me to err and fall into the ditch of lawlessness?

Prayer: Dear Lord, forgive me for assuming I'm exempt from judgment due to my service in Your kingdom. I repent of this and heed Your command to be holy as You are holy. I choose to embrace Your love for me but also the holy fear of You. By choosing both, Your Word promises that I will stay on the highway that leads to life. In Jesus' name, amen.

Profession: I choose to be holy as God is holy!

Children, fear God; that is to say, have a holy awe upon your minds to avoid that which is evil, and a strict care to embrace and do that which is good.

—WILLIAM PENN

17 | DEPART FROM EVIL

The fear of the Lord is a gift from our loving heavenly Father that protects us from departing from Jesus. He is the source of everlasting life, love, joy, peace, goodness, hope, and all its many wonders. To depart from Him is to move toward death, darkness, and eventually the eternal grave. We are told, "By the fear of the LORD one departs from evil" (Proverbs 16:6 NKJV).

Let me share when this truth became real to me. In the late 1980s a popular television evangelist's corruption became widely publicized. He was one of the most well-known individuals in the world, and for the wrong reasons. At the time, his ministry was the largest globally, in both reach and finances, but his mega fame rose when practically every major news source reported daily the saga of his crimes, the ensuing trial, the verdict, and lastly his imprisonment.

He was sentenced to forty-five years in a penitentiary, but a later appeal would see it reduced to five years. In 1994, his fourth year in prison, my assistant received an unexpected phone call. Though I was unknown to him, someone had given him my first book, *Victory in the Wilderness* (now entitled *God, Where are You?!*). He read it in prison and was deeply touched. He asked his assistant to reach out to me to see if I'd come visit him.

I did and will never forget the meeting. He walked into the visiting area in his prison garb. He approached me, stretched out his arms, and gave me an earnest hug that lasted close to a minute. He then grabbed my shoulders, gazed at me with tears, and sincerely asked, "Did you write it or did a ghost writer?"

I responded, "I wrote it. I've experienced suffering, but not near what you've endured."

He then said, "We have so much to talk about and we only have ninety minutes."

I was still a little skittish since it was my first time meeting him. This man had been so maligned and defamed I honestly didn't know who I was talking to. But when we sat down, he disarmed me with his first comment. Gazing into my eyes, he said, "John, this prison was not God's judgment on my life; it was His mercy. If I continued walking the path that I was on, I would have ended up in hell forever."

At that point he had my full attention. He continued to elaborate on how evil he was and how great God's deliverance was in his life. It didn't take long to realize I was speaking to a sincere, broken, and contrite man of God. He proceeded to tell me how God delivered him from darkness the first year of his prison sentence.

I learned each day he spent hours, both personally and in a group, reading the Bible and praying. He enthusiastically shared about their prison church and their pastor, who was a fellow prisoner. Feeling he was the best qualified, I asked why he wasn't the pastor. He explained he wanted no part of leadership until his transformation was complete. He said, "John, I was a master manipulator, and I don't want to give it a chance to resurface."

His statement proved true a year later, for upon his release from prison, he joined a mission organization in downtown Los Angeles. He laid low in the streets for two years caring for the homeless. He loved this because the street people were among the few in the nation who had no idea who he was.

After twenty or so minutes of listening, I felt comfortable enough to ask some questions. I started with the biggest one I could think of: "When did you fall out of love with Jesus?"

I asked this question because earlier in his ministry, his love for Jesus radiated from him. His fire and passion were evident to all who heard him. I wanted to know when his love grew cold and, further, what caused it.

Staring into my eyes, with great sincerity he said, "I didn't fall out of love with Jesus."

I was shocked and a little angered by his comment. *How dare he say this!* I thought. I immediately fired back, "What are you talking about? You committed adultery seven years before you were prosecuted for the mail fraud that ultimately put you in this penitentiary. How can you tell me you loved Jesus those seven years?"

Without breaking eye contact, he calmly said, "John, I loved Jesus the entire time."

My bewilderment was obvious. He paused, then addressed it: "John, I didn't fear God." He paused again, then more fully elaborated, "I loved Jesus, but I didn't fear God."

I was stunned speechless, and quite frankly, was in awe of what had just been stated. There was silence for a good fifteen seconds, my mind processing the entire time. Then he made the statement that still reverberates through my being: "John, there are millions of Americans just like me—they love Jesus, but they don't fear God."

It was as if God had spoken right through his lips. So many questions were suddenly answered by his statement. I was reeling, and the biggest "aha" of the moment was that his story put into words the root cause of the massive departure from faith in our nation. And sadly, the apostasy prevalent then has since escalated.

Scripture makes it clear—the starting place of knowing God intimately is the fear of the Lord. Without it, we develop a phony relationship with a knockoff Jesus—one who is not the Lord of glory. We believe in an unrealistic savior. I will cover this truth in great depth later in the book. But let me first give evidence with two quick examples.

As I write, just this week I was told of the heartbreaking news of a young lady whom I've known since she was a small girl. She was raised in the faith and professed to be a follower of Jesus, but has lived a promiscuous life, with a reputation of being "easy" among her male peers. Recently she posted on Instagram that Jesus held her hand through the entire process of aborting her baby. What Jesus is she referring to?

Another young lady who was married to a godly man told me to my face that Jesus promised her He would take care of her if she decided to divorce her husband. She did and left a wake of devastation with her husband, children, family, and friends. Her reason for divorce wasn't scandalous; she simply didn't love him anymore. No abuse, no immorality, no financial problems—all this came straight from her mouth. In fact, she told me he was a kind and caring husband and father. What Jesus was she referring to?

These are just two of countless examples I could give of those who profess a relationship with Jesus but live in a way that declares otherwise. How are these two, and many others, so deceived? I believe it's the lack of holy fear.

> My dear friends, you have always obeyed God when I was with you. It is even more important that you obey now while I am away from you. Keep on working to complete your salvation with fear and trembling. (Philippians 2:12 NCV)

Paul doesn't write that we should mature in our salvation with *love and kindness.* Many would affirm both these ladies to be loving and kind. They would affirm their years of church attendance and profession of their loyalty to Jesus. But how can they dive headlong into such lawless behavior? They lack what that famous evangelist lacked. It is by the fear of the Lord that we depart from evil, not by the love of God. The love of God draws us to Him; the fear of God keeps us from the evil that seeks to destroy us.

Making It Personal

Passage: All who fear the Lord will hate evil. Therefore, I hate pride and arrogance, corruption and perverse speech. (Proverbs 8:13)

Point: The fear of the Lord is a gift from our loving heavenly Father that protects us from departing from Him. The moment we develop a tolerance for sin, rather than a hate for it, is the moment we begin our departure from Him.

Ponder: Backsliding doesn't occur the moment a person finds themselves in bed with someone they don't have a marriage covenant with. It doesn't start the moment a person finds themselves embezzling money from their employer. It starts long before, when we begin to tolerate what Jesus gave His life to free us from. What do I tolerate that Jesus died to set me free from?

Prayer: Dear Lord, I ask You to forgive me for tolerating sin, not only in my life but in the lives of those believers I'm in relationship with. Forgive me for not gently and with a heart of love confronting them so that they don't continue on the wrong path. I repent of this tolerance. Thank You for forgiving me. In Jesus' name, amen.

Profession: I will love people, for God loves people. I will hate the sin that unmakes the people I love.

My steps have stayed on your path; I have not wavered from following you.

—PSALM 17:5

18 | LONGEVITY

After the two notable experiences in 1994—the church conference where my message on fearing God was corrected and the prison visit with the televangelist—a passion was ignited to understand and grow in holy fear. Both incidents carried a similar message but from two different perspectives.

That church, which was the largest and most influential in the area, no longer exists. And its pastor, who taught that New Testament believers don't need to fear God, is no longer in ministry. The minister I met in prison lost his mega ministry, but since discovering and embracing holy fear, has stayed the course of faithfully serving God and people. He has a different ministry organization presently that's influencing many.

These two unrelated incidents reveal how the fear of the Lord is crucial to avoiding the ensnaring evil that would shorten our tenure as effective ambassadors of Christ. We can sum it up in one word: *longevity*. Recently a respected pastor shared with me his conversation with a Bible university professor, who through extensive research studied individuals in Scripture whom God called and commissioned. He discovered that 75 percent of the chosen messengers had their effectiveness cut short, and many of them didn't finish well. With our present-day ministry tragedies coupled with this minister's research, *longevity* is the challenge we all need to take more seriously.

In the late 1990s, the importance of holy fear regarding *longevity* would be reaffirmed by yet another significant experience and the revelation that would come from it. I was ministering in Kuala Lumpur, Malaysia. It was the tenth and final service, and the meeting was packed with believers who'd traveled from all over the nation. Upon completing the message, many responded to a call to commit to ministry. A crowd four to five deep stood in front of the wide stage waiting for prayer.

I started down the stairs of the platform, when suddenly the presence of God unexpectedly manifested in the auditorium in a tangible and significant way. It was marked by His love and joy. Those in front of me started smiling, which soon turned into laugher, and this joy spread rapidly until everyone up front was affected by it. It seemed Abba Father chose to refresh His children. It didn't take long to figure out I didn't need to do anything, so I just sat on the edge of the platform and enjoyed watching God strengthen and bless His children.

After five to seven minutes, His beautiful presence lifted with a stillness residing in the atmosphere. All of us were quiet and enjoying the remarkable peace in the auditorium. However, within moments God's presence manifested in a different way, one that I'd remembered from Brazil. I stood up anticipating a change. It grew stronger and stronger; there was no wind blowing this time, but His authority and awesomeness were unmistakably real. Those who were laughing moments earlier, without any spoken direction, broke out almost simultaneously crying and weeping, some of them profusely.

The presence grew stronger, and the weeping intensified. It was as if these quiet Asian people were being baptized in the fire of God. Again, it's not possible to describe the manifestation, and that's not the point of sharing this sacred moment, but what's important is the awesomeness of His presence. It increased to the point I didn't think we could take any more.

In this encounter, I became keenly aware of the difference between our soul and spirit. We are told the Word of God cuts "between soul and spirit" (Hebrews 4:12). My mind (soul) was thinking, *I can't handle any more! God, it's too much!* Yet my heart (spirit) was crying out, *God, please don't lift, please don't stop!*

Once again, I had the thought, *John Bevere, you make one wrong move, you say one wrong word, you're dead.* As in Brazil, I can't say for sure this would've happened, but I knew irreverence wouldn't be tolerated in this atmosphere.

The entire manifestation of His awesome presence lasted three to four minutes and then lifted. Once it did, without any direction given, the people became quiet in unison again. I remained silent for several minutes in the calm and peace of the aftermath.

As we were leaving the building, the environment was solemn, quiet, and reverent. I stopped to engage a man and his wife from India; both were significantly impacted by God's presence. We just looked at one another in amazement and silence for a few moments, then she softly spoke: "John, I feel so clean inside." Her husband nodded in agreement.

When she said these words, my heart leapt. Finally, someone articulated accurately what I had felt afterward in Brazil, and now in Malaysia. I responded with controlled emotion, "I do too." We didn't converse any longer, but her statement continued to reverberate in me the rest of the evening.

The next morning, I was in my hotel room getting ready to play basketball with the young men on the ministry staff of the church and Bible school. Suddenly, I heard the Holy Spirit say to my heart, "Son, read Psalm 19."

I grabbed my Bible, opened to the passage, and started reading. Once I reached verse 9, I read:

The fear of the LORD is *clean, enduring forever.* (Psalm 19:9 NKJV)

I shouted in my room, "That's it! There it is!" I was in awe; this is exactly what the woman had said to me the day before. There was an indescribable cleanness, a profound purity we sensed in our souls.

Then the words "enduring forever" leapt off the page. The Holy Spirit immediately spoke to my heart:

Son, Lucifer led worship right before My throne, he led the entire hosts of heaven as he was ordained and anointed to do so. He was close to Me, beheld My glory, but didn't fear Me; therefore, he didn't endure before My throne forever. (Ezekiel 28:13–17)

One-third of the angels beheld My glory, aligned themselves with Lucifer. They didn't fear Me, they didn't endure in My presence forever. (Revelation 12:4, 7)

Adam and Eve walked in the presence of My glory in the cool of the day. They didn't fear Me, they didn't endure in the garden of Eden forever.

Son, every created being who surrounds My throne for all eternity will have passed the holy test of the fear of the Lord. (Genesis 3:8)

My eyes were opened to this truth. I began to think of all the pastors whose ministry effectiveness has been cut short or who didn't finish well. Many started passionately, loved Jesus dearly, obeyed and sacrificed to minister to God's people, but they became jaded, cynical, and many left ministry. They didn't endure.

Others were still in ministry but were using it as a means of gain and various other self-seeking purposes. Some would become sex predators, using their leadership positions to target innocent women; some would become consultants and charge hefty amounts to craft deceitful messages for ministers to manipulate their followers to give large offerings; others would lie about prophetic words from God, figuring out ways of ciphering information from the individuals they were supposedly ministering to, and then proclaiming it as if it were revealed by God. The list of corruptive behavior is almost endless.

How do those who start out so pure end up so polluted? Why isn't there longevity of effectiveness? It's the lack of holy fear. What Jesus delighted in is taken for granted or even shunned, as was the case of the pastor in the southeastern United States. What God calls "His treasure," they talk themselves and others out of. But listen to God's Word regarding holy fear and longevity:

How joyful are those who fear the LORD . . . Their good deeds will last forever. Such people . . . will long be remembered. (Psalm 112:1, 3, 6)

We don't have to experience tragedies to discover how important holy fear is. Please, for the sake of God's glory and your longevity, make holy fear your treasure.

Making It Personal

Passage: The love of the LORD remains forever with those who fear him. (Psalm 103:17)

Point: Every created being who surrounds God's throne for eternity will be those who fear Him.

Ponder: One of the aspects of living well is finishing well. The fear of the Lord endures forever. How can I make holy fear a staple in my life? What practical ways can I keep holy fear as a filter in all I say or do?

Prayer: Dear heavenly Father, Your Word states that You are able to keep me from falling away and will bring me with great joy into Your glorious presence without a single fault. I know it's by the redemptive work of my Lord Jesus accompanied by embracing holy fear that secures this eternal relationship. I ask that holy fear would abide within me always that I may forever live in Your presence. I ask this in Jesus' name, amen.

Profession: In holy fear I will abide in the house of the Lord, in His presence, forever.

If you don't delight in the fact that your Father is holy, holy, holy, then you are spiritually dead. You may be in a church. You may go to a Christian school. But if there is no delight in your soul for the holiness of God, you don't know God. You don't love God. You're out of touch with God. You're asleep to his character.

—R. C. SPROUL

19 | CLEANSE OURSELVES

"The fear of the LORD is *clean, enduring forever*" (Psalm 19:9 NKJV). The psalmist gives two remarkable fruits of holy fear that should not be overlooked or taken lightly: *cleanliness* and *longevity*. Let's examine the first, and we'll further address the latter in a future chapter. Paul writes:

> Therefore, having these promises, beloved, let us *cleanse ourselves* from all filthiness of the flesh and spirit, perfecting *holiness* in the fear of God. (2 Corinthians 7:1 NKJV)

Here we see the same truth the psalmist communicates, yet in more depth. I first want to point out that holiness is brought to maturity through the fear of the Lord, not the love of God. Recall the popular evangelist who lived an ungodly lifestyle, while at the same time loving Jesus. Once he embraced holy fear, he cleansed himself and walked free from former impurities. This in turn led him to a more authentic relationship with Jesus, one greater than he'd known before. What he learned experientially we also see in Scripture.

As we've already discussed, holiness is not the most popular subject these days. For many it carries a bad taste because it's no fun and puts a damper on life. It's viewed as either legalistic bondage or a virtue that's noble but unattainable. C. S. Lewis addressed this ignorance by writing, "How little people know who think that holiness is dull. When one meets the real thing . . . it is irresistible."[1] So prepare yourself for the irresistible as we dive in.

As I mentioned before, the primary definition of holiness is "separation unto God," and this certainly includes purity. Consider a bride. She sets herself apart for her husband, which includes refusing to desire or engage with other lovers. This represents the purity aspect of holiness. Even so, Paul tells us to cleanse ourselves. He doesn't say, "The blood of Jesus will cleanse us." However, let me make this point clear: the blood of Jesus does indeed cleanse us from all sin; however, we get confused when we mix the work of *justification* with the work of *sanctification*.

When we repented and received Jesus Christ as our Lord, our sins were forgiven, and we were washed completely clean. God buried our sins in the sea of forgetfulness. He doesn't remember them! This work is complete, perfect, and cannot be improved upon. We did nothing to merit this amazing reality; it was a gift from God. This is the work of *justification*.

But the very moment we received justification, the work of *sanctification* (holiness) began. This is when what was done on the inside of us is *worked out*; our new nature becomes an outward reality in the way we live. This is precisely what Paul addresses when he writes:

Work out your own salvation with fear and trembling; for it is God who works in you both *to will* and *to do* for His good pleasure. (Philippians 2:12–13 NKJV)

Clearly, it's still a work of God's grace, but we must cooperate with the power He gives both *to will* and *to do*. Just as fear and trembling positioned the people of Brazil to enter God's presence and receive from Him, so holy fear and trembling ignite and position us to be empowered by His grace for obedience.

A common mistake of many teachers in the Western church is declaring the work of holiness to be the same as the work of justification. In other words, we don't need to do anything; Jesus did it all. So the argument is, even though we continue to live no differently from the world, controlled by our various lusts, we are holy because Jesus is our holiness. What makes this even trickier is there are indeed scriptures that seem to support their claims in the New Testament. However, their error stems from confusing our *positional* holiness with our *behavioral* holiness. Allow me to explain.

Positional holiness is solely due to what Jesus did for us and speaks of our position in Christ; it's one of the blessings of Christ's work of justification: "Even before he made the world, God loved us and chose us in Christ *to be holy* and without fault in his eyes" (Ephesians 1:4). We never could have earned this position. Again, Paul writes, "Christ made us right with God; he made us pure and holy, and he freed us from sin" (1 Corinthians 1:30).

On October 2, 1982, Lisa Toscano and I entered a marriage covenant, and she became Lisa Bevere. On that very day she took the *position* of my wife. She's not more my wife today than the day I married her, nor will she be more my wife forty years from now. Positionally, she fully became my wife on that wedding day; the work was complete. Similarly, in Christ we were made holy and clean on the day of our salvation, and we will never be more holy.

However, once Lisa became my wife, her *behavior* began to align with her position. Before she was my wife, she dated other guys, gave them her phone number, lived for her own desires, and all the other things single women do, but now she didn't do these things any longer. Her actions aligned with the covenant we made together. This behavior has grown more mature in aligning with our covenant the longer we've been married. Listen to what the apostle Peter writes:

> [Live] as children of obedience [to God]; do not conform yourselves to
> the evil desires [that governed you] in your former ignorance [when you
> did not know the requirements of the Gospel]. But as the One Who called
> you is holy, you yourselves also be holy in all your *conduct and manner*

of living. For it is written, You shall be holy, for I am holy. (1 Peter 1:14–16 AMPC)

Notice Peter is not addressing our *positional* holiness; rather he speaks of our *behavioral* holiness, which is exactly what Paul addresses when he tells us to cleanse ourselves from all filthiness. This is the process of sanctification, not the free positional gift of being justified.

Are there other scriptures written in the New Testament addressing our behavioral holiness? The answer is yes. There are far too many to list, but let me cite another:

God's will is for you to be holy, so stay away from all sexual sin. Then each of you will *control his own body* and live in holiness and honor—not in lustful passion like the pagans who do not know God and his ways. (1 Thessalonians 4:3–5)

Recently after a Sunday morning service, a man said to me, "I'm a single Christian. I sleep with women because it's impossible to live a celibate life. I stop for a few months, but then return to sleeping with women. But that isn't the main issue of what I'm here to talk about. My main question is, why am I having so many struggles in my business?"

I was in shock. Have our unbalanced messages of grace brought people to the place of believing they will abide in God's presence and blessings while they live in flagrant sin? In a Q&A at a church women's conference, a lady asked my wife, "I really love my husband, but he travels a lot, and I keep sleeping with other men. What should I do? Should I tell him?"

These two really believe they are in relationship with Jesus—but is it the Jesus at the right hand of God or is it a *knockoff* Jesus? These examples are only the tip of the iceberg; I've had far too many similar encounters with other individuals. Is the call to live a holy life so muted that all conviction has been silenced? Yet Paul writes, "Whoever rejects this teaching is not rejecting a human being, but God, who gives you his Holy Spirit" (1 Thessalonians 4:8 GNT).

Keep in mind, there is an irresistible aspect of holiness, and we will see this clearly as we continue in our pursuit of it.

═══════ Making It Personal ═══════

Passage: If someone claims, "I know God," but doesn't obey God's commandments, that person is a liar and is not living in the truth. (1 John 2:4)

Point: The work of sanctification (holiness) is when what was done on the inside of us is worked out; our new nature becomes an outward reality in the way we live.

Ponder: Holiness is a work of God's grace, but I must cooperate with the power He gives both to will and to do what He desires of me. Do I believe this? Have I ignored this truth and His command to live holy because I have confused positional holiness with behavioral holiness? Or have I allowed past failures to stifle my faith in God's empowering work within me? How can I return to believing this, so it becomes a reality in my life?

Prayer: Dear heavenly Father, I ask that You work in me both to will and accomplish Your good pleasure. I desire to live outwardly what You've already done for me inwardly. In Jesus' name, amen.

Profession: I am working out my salvation with holy fear and trembling.

Mark out a straight path
for your feet ... and work
at living a holy life.

—HEBREWS 12:13–14

20 | OUR PURSUIT

Holiness is not an end unto itself; rather, it's a passageway into what's most important. Let's now turn to the irresistible aspect of it by examining our opening scripture from a different translation:

> Pursue . . . holiness, without which no one will see the Lord. (Hebrews 12:14 NKJV)

The word "pursue" is the Greek word *diōkō*, which is defined as "to do something with intense effort and with definite purpose or goal."[1] In looking at both translations and hearing *diōkō*'s definition, there's no question, this statement speaks of passionately chasing after holiness with the intent to apprehend it.

Our first question should be, Is this *positional* holiness or *behavioral* holiness? Let's revert to the example of Lisa's and my marriage. Can you imagine Lisa saying to one of her close friends, "I'm chasing with intense effort to be John's wife!"

Her friend would laugh and say, "You already are! You became his wife on the day of your marriage."

A woman doesn't chase after the *position* of "wife" that she already holds. But a woman can pursue the optimal *behavior* of a wife. It's the same with holiness—we don't chase after a *position* we already hold, but rather the *behavior* "worthy of the Lord" (Colossians 1:10 NKJV).

We are told with certainty that the consequence for ignoring this command is *not seeing the Lord*. That is a sobering thought! It certainly affects us eternally, but that's not the focus of our discussion at this time. What is important to the topic at hand is, how does this affect us in the here and now?

Since I'm a citizen of the United States of America, I could say I have a "relationship" with the president. I am under his governing authority and am affected by the decisions he makes, as are 332 million other American citizens. But even though I have this relationship with the president, to this day I've not been granted a private audience with one. Simply put, I've not been in the presence of or interacted with any of our US presidents.

On the other hand, there are other Americans who do get to *see* the president on a regular basis; they are his friends or work closely with him. In either case, they know the man who lives in the White House much better than I do. They know him on an intimate level; I only know him as our nation's leader.

Similarly, there are millions of believers who are under the rulership of Jesus Christ. He protects, loves, and provides for them and answers their requests. However, the question is, do they *see* Him? In other words, do they experience His *manifest presence*?

The multiple thousands of believers in Brazil lacked the behavior that would bring them into the presence of the Lord. Once they repented, they were granted an audience with the King. This holds true daily, and even on a moment-by-moment basis. If we lack godly fear, we lack the drive to pursue the holy behavior granting us the privilege of His manifest presence. Jesus says, "He who has My commandments and keeps them . . . I will love him and manifest Myself to him" (John 14:21 NKJV).

It's worth repeating: *no behavioral holiness, no seeing the Lord*. Why is this so critical? First, if we don't see Him—if we lack His manifest presence—we can't know Him intimately. We can only know *about* Him, not unlike my relationship with United States presidents. Or worse, we deceive ourselves by creating a fictional Jesus. This illusion is most dangerous because we believe we know Someone we don't. James tells us, "But don't just listen to God's word. You must do what it says. Otherwise, you are only fooling yourselves" (James 1:22). One who is fooled believes they know someone or something, but in reality, they don't.

The second reason is equally important. Without beholding Him—not being in His presence—we cannot be changed or transformed into His likeness. Paul mentions that those who see the Lord "are being transformed into the same image from one degree of glory to another" (2 Corinthians 3:18 ESV). This transformation begins within and subsequently works out to where it is witnessed by others.

Our purity cannot be like the Pharisees'. Jesus said, "Outwardly you look like righteous people, but inwardly your hearts are filled with hypocrisy and lawlessness" (Matthew 23:28). Their motives were as impure and filthy as dead corpses. They lacked the fear of the Lord, which in turn caused them to pursue a righteousness that was strictly based on outward behavior, making their projected image the focus. This prevented the inner transformation that brings forth corresponding outward behavior. They believed they knew God, but the reality is they didn't know their Creator who stood before them, and consequently were out of step with His wishes. They fooled themselves.

Even so today, the holiness we pursue must originate in our hearts—our thoughts, motives, and intentions. This will ultimately drive our outward behavior. This is why Jesus says, "Blessed are the pure in heart, for they shall see God" (Matthew 5:8 NKJV). Without seeing Him, we lack inner transformation—authentic holiness—and consequently we don't see Him. It's cyclical.

It's not enough to have an outward form of godliness but deny the power of the transformation of our inward desires. We must long for truth in our inward parts (motives and intentions); that must be our pursuit. The apostle James is very strong with believers who take holiness lightly. He writes:

Your motives are all wrong—you want only what will give you pleasure. You *adulterers*! Don't you realize that friendship with the world makes you an enemy of God? (James 4:3–4)

James uses the word *adulterers*, a term used for the violation of a marriage covenant. God often uses marriage imagery to illustrate our covenant with Him; Jesus is called the groom, and we are His bride. Paul states that a marriage between a man and woman is an example of the way Jesus Christ and the church are united (Ephesians 5:31–32).

The world lives for selfish gain or prideful achievements and therefore focuses on projected and perceived images. When we align ourselves with the world's desires in our neglect of pursuing holiness, we become adulterers. It's such an affront to our Husband that we actually turn ourselves into His enemies. Therefore, James goes on to say: "Purify your hearts, for your loyalty is divided between God and the world" (James 4:8). We can only purify our hearts by embracing the fear of the Lord, which drives us to pursue authentic holiness!

I've been married to Lisa for more than forty years, and there are strong reasons I've not committed adultery against her. The first and foremost is that I fear God. I made a covenant with Him to love and nurture her regardless of her response or behavior.

The second reason is because I don't want to lose intimacy with this magnificent woman. I love that she confides in me, sharing her innermost secrets and the longings of her heart. In essence, I love our closeness.

It's no different with Jesus. The reason I passionately avoid committing adultery against Him is that I don't want to lose the intimacy we share. I love the closeness of His presence and the intimate conversations we have together. I love it when He shares secrets with me that I've never known before. That could be why we are told:

The *secret of the Lord* is with those who fear Him, and He will show them His covenant. (Psalm 25:14 NKJV)

We are now just beginning to discover the irresistible aspect of holiness. We'll continue unveiling its beauty in the next chapter.

Making It Personal

Passage: Whoever loves a pure heart and gracious speech will have the king as a friend. (Proverbs 22:11)

Point: Without chasing after behavioral holiness with the intent to apprehend, we cannot enter into the presence of the Lord. It's not about when we arrive at the place of perfect holiness but rather when we make it our heart's pursuit.

Ponder: God knows if I am chasing after holy behavior or if I'm consistently excusing my love or tolerance for worldly desires and the pride of accomplishments. It all begins with my heart's intentions. Will I chase after purity of heart and mind, resulting in a change of actions? Will I do so even if those who are close to me don't?

Prayer: Dear heavenly Father, forgive me for not pursuing holiness. I've ignored its importance, but now I see that it is to be my pursuit, for it is the doorway to an audience with You. Please forgive my worldly behavior and pursuits and cleanse me with the blood of Jesus. I repent of my casual attitude toward holiness, in Jesus' name, amen.

Profession: I am chasing after holiness with the full intent to apprehend it. My goal is to be holy as God is holy.

But for those who are righteous, the way is not steep and rough. You are a God who does what is right, and you smooth out the path ahead of them.

—ISAIAH 26:7

21 | DESIRE AND POWER

Perhaps at this point you are lamenting the fact that you've *tried* to live a holy life but, quite honestly, have failed more than you've succeeded. You long for intimacy with God, but you've struggled with obedience. Please know this up front: He longs for you more than you long for Him. Rejoice, for God is for you! Let this truth alleviate the tension.

There's a good chance the problem lies in the fact that you have *tried*. The law of Moses proved our inability to keep God's commands; we require divine help. This needed assistance is none other than God's grace. Most believers know the grace of Jesus Christ frees us from the law's requirements, but what many don't know is that it goes one step further: it grants us a new nature, giving us the potential to live free from sin (Romans 6:6–7).

If we look at Paul's command to cleanse ourselves from all filthiness of the flesh and spirit, it is preceded by a statement often overlooked. A few paragraphs before that he writes:

We then, as workers together with Him also plead with you not to receive the grace of God in vain. For He says: "In an acceptable time . . . I have helped you." (2 Corinthians 6:1–2 NKJV)

The acceptable time has come; we can live a holy life with His help. Sadly, God's grace has been communicated far below its potential. It's been taught as eternal salvation, forgiveness of sin, freedom from the penalty of sin, and an unmerited gift. While these realities are completely true, what has not been communicated as widely is its empowerment. God speaks to the apostle Paul: "My grace is all you need. My power works best in weakness" (2 Corinthians 12:9). Simply put, "Paul, what you couldn't do in your own ability, you can do now by My power, which is called grace."

Peter affirms this truth: "Grace . . . be multiplied to you . . . as His divine power [grace] has given to us all things that pertain to life and godliness" (2 Peter 1:2–3 NKJV). The NLT version is even more direct, "By his divine power [grace], God has given us everything we need for living a godly life." Grace empowers us to live holy!

Why is this truth so vital? Christianity is a life of faith. The entire message is called the "word of faith" (Romans 10:8 NKJV). In other words, we will not receive anything from God unless we believe, and we cannot believe what we do not know. So if we're unaware of grace's empowerment, we will continue to attempt to please God in our own ability. And that would lead to a fruitless, miserable existence.

Consider the example of the new birth. There are many unsaved people who confess their belief that God can save. However, until they repent and believe in the gospel, they are without saving grace. The same proves true for our pursuit of holiness. There are many Christians who believe that God can give the ability to live holy, but until they wholeheartedly believe that *grace empowers*, they won't benefit.

Paul pleads with the Corinthian believers "not to receive the grace of God in vain" (2 Corinthians 6:1 NKJV). What does it mean to receive something in vain? It simply means to not utilize it to its fullest potential. If a man is given farming equipment, along with seeds, he can grow food to eat and live on. But if he doesn't use what's been provided, he'll lose his life to starvation. After he dies, what will his neighbors say? "He received the equipment and seeds in vain."

This is what Paul is addressing—God has given grace to help you live in a way you couldn't in your own ability. It empowers you to pursue and attain a holy lifestyle. Don't neglect tapping into this power because of unbelief.

If God's grace is merely what's been widely taught in Western culture—no more than salvation, forgiveness, and a ticket to heaven—how could anyone ever receive it in vain? There's no potential to be wasted, so Paul's statement makes no sense.

If we follow the apostle's train of thought, it all adds up. The Corinthian church was worldly; they were found lacking in their quest for holiness. To confirm this point, Paul writes a little later in the same letter, "Many of you have not given up your old sins. You have not repented of your impurity, sexual immorality, and eagerness for lustful pleasure" (2 Corinthians 12:21). Back in chapter 6, Paul starts out by pleading for these believers to not waste God's grace, then interjects his love for them and asks why it's not being reciprocated. Then he returns to the main thought, how their neglect of God's grace was evident by the ungodly people who influenced them:

> You are not the same as those who do not believe. So do not join yourselves to them. Good and bad do not belong together. Light and darkness cannot share together. (2 Corinthians 6:14 NCV)

We must remember, there's a difference between going into the world to reach unbelievers and being influenced by an improper alignment with them. This will only result in behavior that can remove us from the path of life. Again, this is identified as spiritual adultery.

Paul then reminds these carnal believers that they are God's dwelling place and that His desire is to "live in them and walk among them. I will be their God, and they will be my people. Therefore, come out from among unbelievers, and separate yourselves from them, says the LORD. Don't touch their filthy things, *and I will welcome you*" (2 Corinthians 6:16–17).

Again, we see that the promise of God's manifest presence, but at an even greater level. He's not speaking of periodically visiting us but of dwelling in and with us! Once again we see the promise of *seeing God* (His manifest presence) is conditional. If we stay clear from the selfish and prideful desires that the world clings to, we are promised an enduring audience with the King—"and I will welcome you." The converse is also true: if we contaminate ourselves with the filth of the world, we're not granted an audience. Paul concludes with the focused statement:

> Having, then, these promises, beloved, may we cleanse ourselves from every pollution of flesh and spirit, perfecting sanctification in the fear of God. (2 Corinthians 7:1 YLT)

Now we can more fully understand Paul's statement to the Philippian church: "Work out your own salvation with fear and trembling; for it is God who works in you both *to will* and *to do* for His good pleasure" (Philippians 2:12–13 NKJV). The fear of the Lord motivates us *to will* (gives us the desire), and the grace of our Lord Jesus Christ enables us *to do* (empowers us).

Taking it one step further, where there's a lack of desire (due to a lack of holy fear), empowerment will not be a priority and thus will not be utilized; it will be received in vain! This is why holy fear is so critical to our effectiveness and longevity.

Hopefully it's become clear that purity is a huge aspect of holiness but not its full definition. Again, the primary definition of holiness is to be *consecrated to Him*, to be *completely His*. Let's give a fuller illustration of the core meaning of holiness: When a bride marries a groom, she gives herself entirely to him. Included in this consecration is a purity in both her position and her behavior. Purity is not the ultimate goal; it's being a consecrated bride for her groom, which includes purity.

Therefore, true holiness is a transcendent, consecrated purity, one that opens the door to deep intimacy with God. This is the *irresistible* we will continue to discuss before the conclusion of this book. But first we need to continue our discussion of what it practically looks like to live consecrated to our Groom. The answer is found in one word: *obedience*.

Making It Personal

Passage: Be strong in the grace that is in Christ Jesus. (2 Timothy 2:1 NKJV)

Point: If we're unaware of grace's empowerment, we will continue to attempt to please God in our own ability. We will have received God's grace in vain.

Ponder: Have I *tried* to live a holy life and failed more than I've succeeded? Have I attempted in my own ability? Have I depended on God's grace to empower me to live holy? If not, how can I change this?

Prayer: Dear heavenly Father, I realize that it's only by the power of Your grace that I can live a godly life, one that welcomes Your glorious presence. Forgive me for attempting to do this in my own ability. From this moment forward I will be strong in Your grace to live a set-apart life that glorifies Jesus. In Jesus' name I pray, amen.

Profession: I am motivated by holy fear to pursue holiness and will accomplish it by the power of God's grace.

Our Response to God's Word

WEEK 4

Make me walk along the path of your commands, for that is where my happiness is found.

—PSALM 119:35

22 | TREMBLING AT GOD'S WORD

In our first section it was stated that the fear of the Lord can be broken into two categorical definitions: to tremble at God's presence and to tremble at His Word. We've discussed God's glorious presence, although far from exhaustively, for we will be continually awed by it throughout eternity. In this section we'll turn our focus toward how we respond to His Word.

To begin, let's consider a time period when God's people drifted from a genuine relationship with Him and replaced it with mere formalities. To get their attention God asks: "Heaven is my throne, and the earth is my footstool. Could you build me a temple as good as that?" (Isaiah 66:1).

If we read the first five verses of this chapter in context, we find the Almighty addressing people who have attempted to develop and maintain a relationship with Him on their own terms. They've halfheartedly adhered to His ways under the assumption it would appease Him. God makes it clear that their chosen path is offensive, but straightaway He gives what's required to enter an authentic relationship:

"I will bless those who have humble and contrite hearts, who *tremble at my word.*" (Isaiah 66:2)

The phrase "I will bless" is the Hebrew verb *nabat*, which is defined as "to look, to watch, to regard. It has the sense of looking somewhat intensely in a focused way at something." God, in essence, is saying, "This is the person whom I will pay close attention to." Three virtues are listed: humility, a contrite heart, and those who "tremble at my word," which will be our focus in this section.

The one who trembles at God's Word always exalts what He says above anything else. Nothing is more important. It's the true evidence of holy fear. This person is most blessed. In the same light Paul writes:

> My beloved, as you have always obeyed, *not as in my presence only*, but now *much more in my absence*, work out your own salvation with fear and trembling. (Philippians 2:12 NKJV)

Think of this statement not as Paul writing to the believers in Philippi but as God speaking directly to us. Focus on the words "always obeyed"; it means unconditional. This would apply to whether you sense His presence or not, whether you see Him moving on your behalf or not, whether your prayer is answered in your expected time frame or not.

It is easy to obey God when you are in a conference setting, where people are kind to one another and the presence of God is strong. But what about when a trusted team member lies about you and you're fired from your position? Will you forgive according to His Word or retaliate to get even?

What if you're on a business trip and feeling lonely, and then you start to recall that your spouse has been critical of you. A good-looking team member of the opposite sex compliments you, speaks to your need, then seductively offers to spend the evening together in the hotel room. No one will find out. Will you flee or accept?

What if you're working late on your computer, surfing the web for needed information for your job, when you run across porn? Do you engage?

These are incidents when God's presence seems absent. If you tremble at His Word, you will obey no matter the circumstances because there is no greater precedence. This indicates you walk in holy fear, for "by the fear of the LORD one departs from evil" (Proverbs 16:6 NKJV).

The psalmist writes:

Blessed is the man who fears the LORD, who delights greatly in His commandments. (Psalm 112:1 NKJV)

The God-fearing man or woman not only obeys but greatly delights in doing so. Obedience is not a burden; it's a joy. This person has the foundational understanding that God is our Creator, and therefore He knows what makes us and what undoes us.

I remember when our four sons were toddlers. Christmas day was basically a workday. Most dads with small children understand what I'm about to say. Once all the presents were opened, there were gifts that needed to be assembled. I was the typical dad; I'd open the box, pour out the pieces on the floor, toss the box and instruction manual aside, and start building. Depending on the gift, usually after an hour or so, I was finished, but to my surprise, there would still be ten pieces sitting on the floor. I'd flip the 'On' switch, and nothing would happen. What would I do? I'd search for the instruction manual, grab it, deconstruct the toy, and rebuild it according to the manufacturer's manual. And behold, it would work!

The person who fears God always obeys. This person, at the core of his or her being, is unmovable from the following foundational truths:

1. God is the One who knows what's right for me.
2. God is pure love, and I am the focus of His love.
3. God will never tell me to do anything that is detrimental. Whatever He says will always end up best.
4. Therefore, no matter what He says, I gladly choose to obey.

The children of Israel complained constantly. They were displeased with how they were led and what was transpiring in their lives. They blamed God for their discomfort, lack, and anything else that wasn't gratifying. They lacked holy fear and didn't tremble at His Word. God spoke:

> Because you did not serve the LORD your God with *joy* and *gladness of heart*, for the abundance of everything, therefore you shall serve your enemies. (Deuteronomy 28:47–48 NKJV)

Trembling at His Word involves joy and gladness in the core of our being. If absent, it's only a matter of time before circumstances reveal the lack of joy. I will never forget the time I discovered the five sins that kept Israel from its destiny: craving evil things, worshiping idols, sexual immorality, testing God, and complaining (1 Corinthians 10:6–10). When I read "complaining," I about hit the ceiling! I cried out, "What? Complaining! How can complaining be in a list with these other *massive* sins?"

I heard the Holy Spirit say, "Son, complaining is a serious sin in My eyes." He showed me that complaining protests, "God, I don't like what You are doing in my life, and if I were You I would do it differently."

He then said, "It is an affront to My character, it's rebellion to My will, and overall, it's a gross lack of holy fear."

I shared this with Lisa, and we agreed to discipline our children for complaining with the understanding it was rebellion. I took it seriously. I shunned murmuring and grumbling of any sort and made sure to never utter a word of complaint. However, later, while on a four-day fast, I heard the Holy Spirit whisper, "Son, I hear the complaining in your heart."

I immediately fell to my knees, repenting. God later showed me that I was not serving the Lord with *joy* and *gladness of heart*, and my enemies had the upper hand. Let's look at Paul's words again:

> My beloved, as you have always obeyed, not as in my presence only, but now much more in my absence, work out your own salvation with fear and trembling; for it is God who works in you both to will and to do for *His* good pleasure. *Do all things without complaining.* (Philippians 2:12–14 NKJV)

It was shortly after this four-day fast that I discovered the depth of what is stated in this scripture. It opened my eyes to the fact that complaining is the antithesis of holy fear; it's not *trembling at His Word*. We dishonor God and His Word when we think or speak from the posture of discontent.

Those who fear God are firmly established that there's nothing more important or beneficial than obedience. They obey no matter the cost and don't filter God's Word through the culture or trends of present-day society. They also don't base their obedience to God's Word on how other believers behave; they simply obey.

Making It Personal

Passage: If you are *willing* and *obedient*, you shall eat the good of the land. (Isaiah 1:19 NKJV)

Point: The evidence of holy fear is obedience, which entails both a right attitude and follow-through in action, no matter the circumstances.

Ponder: Do I only obey when conditions are favorable? Do I tend to complain when it's not going my way? How can I maintain an attitude of joy and gratitude at all times? How can I firm up my resolve to obey?

Prayer: Dear heavenly Father, forgive my lack of trembling at Your Word. My obedience has been conditional, and my attitude hasn't been one of joy and gratitude. I repent and ask Your forgiveness. I embrace holy fear. Please teach and empower me to obey at all times with an attitude of joy. In Jesus' name I pray, amen.

Profession: I fear God and therefore He is working in me both to will and to do His good pleasure.

It is better to tremble at the word of the Lord, and to bow before the infinite majesty of divine love, than to shout oneself hoarse.

—C. H. SPURGEON

23 | IMMEDIATELY

A major attribute of godly fear is unconditional obedience to His Word, which will have startling benefits in our lives. There are five distinct aspects of trembling at God's Word, and over the next five days we'll look at them individually. Here's the first:

1. Obey God immediately.

Obedience is a premium for those who fear God. They don't put personal interests before fulfilling what God has told them to do. Holy fear instills in our hearts that *what's important to God is priority to me*.

There are numerous scriptures we could look at, but to set a precedence, we'll look at two statements from Jesus:

> This is how I want you to conduct yourself in these matters. If you enter your place of worship and, about to make an offering, you suddenly remember a grudge a friend has against you, abandon your offering, leave *immediately*, go to this friend and make things right. Then and only then, come back and work things out with God. (Matthew 5:23–24 MSG)

Notice the word *immediately*. Again, as in Isaiah 66, Jesus emphasizes that we shouldn't initiate "doing something for God" while neglecting to obey what He has already told us to do. Jesus addresses the specific situation of holding a grudge, but the general principal applies to all circumstances.

Recall the man who shared with me his repetitive pattern of fornication, and yet he was puzzled by his unanswered prayers and wondering why his business was not succeeding as he hoped. Let's pause and think this through. If it wasn't his priority to obey God's Word to flee sexual immorality, why would he expect God's priority to be to bless his business?

Eli, the head priest of Israel, had two sons who were also priests under his leadership, but these sons were wicked. They committed adultery and took offerings by force. Eli *delayed* properly addressing his sons' wickedness. The Lord's response to his neglect: "Why do you give your sons more honor than you give me?" (1 Samuel 2:29).

When we are slow or neglect to obey God for any person or purpose, we honor that person or purpose above honoring God. It's a lack of holy fear. God then says:

"I will honor those who honor me, and I will *despise* those who *think lightly* of me." (1 Samuel 2:30)

These are sobering words. We *think lightly* of God when we delay or neglect to obey His Word. We in essence communicate: He's not our priority. God says He will *despise* those who *think lightly* of Him. The word *despise* is not the best-translated word. It is the Hebrew word *qālal*, which is defined "to be slight, to be *trivial*." *Trivial* means of little worth or importance. One way this statement could be interpreted is that God views as *trivial* what's important to us who think lightly of His Word. No one in their right mind would desire this scenario.

If the businessman would have honored God's Word for sexual purity, perhaps God would have viewed his business as important. Instead, it seems to be a trivial matter.

Another passage that illustrates the importance of immediate obedience is Jesus' words to the church in Ephesus:

Repent and do the first works, or else I will come to you *quickly* and remove your lampstand from its place—unless you repent. (Revelation 2:5 NKJV)

To repent means to change the way you think—and thus act—in order to come in line with God's Word. If this church delayed its obedience, they would miss their window of opportunity to remain blessed. Jesus would come *quickly* and remove their influence. Again, this is a sobering thought.

In Luke's gospel we are told a story illustrating missed opportunities due to timing and priorities. Jesus said, "A man prepared a great feast and sent out many invitations. When the banquet was ready, he sent his servant to tell the guests, 'Come, the banquet is ready'" (Luke 14:16–17). No doubt, it's the Word of the Lord: the feast is ready! Timing is of the essence.

Look at the response of those invited, "But they all began making excuses" (v. 18). Seemingly sound reasons are given for their inability to attend. One had bought land, one needed to attend to his business, and the other had a wife who needed his attention. The excuses didn't include adultery, stealing, murder, or anything else we would classify as sinful. However, *when what is not sin takes precedence over the Word of the Lord, it becomes sin.*

The servant came back with the report of those who were invited, and we read, "His master was furious" (v. 21). Not unhappy but furious. Why? Because his invitation was taken lightly; it wasn't priority.

What does the master do? He invites others who were not originally invited. Jesus concludes with: "For none of those I first invited will get even the smallest taste of my banquet" (v. 24). Their window of opportunity was missed. Their excuses seemed harmless, but it's important to remember that even harmless things can detour us from fulfilling God's will. This easily occurs when the fear of the Lord is absent from our hearts.

Many more missed opportunities are recorded in Scripture that were the result of delayed obedience—in fact, too many to list—but I'll select one more that's riveting. In Luke 9, Jesus invites two different men to "Follow Me." What an invitation—the Lord of all creation invites you to walk with

Him! The first man *agreed*, but with a condition: "Lord, *first* let me return home and bury my father" (v. 59).

The man *agreed* to follow Jesus, but he *delayed* it by putting his personal interests first. Scholars tell us in those times when a firstborn son buried his father he received a double portion of the inheritance, while the other sons received a single portion. However, if he didn't fulfill his duty, it would fall to the secondborn. His excuse seemed legitimate, and the delay didn't fall under the category of sin. However, he was left behind. Sadly, it was a missed opportunity.

The other man was given the same invitation, to which he responded, "Yes, Lord, I will follow you, but *first* let me say good-bye to my family" (v. 61). Again, we hear the word *first*; and again, his reason for delay wouldn't be considered sinful. Still, he missed his window of opportunity to be close to the Creator of the heavens and earth.

In the following chapter we read, "After these things the Lord appointed seventy others also, and sent them two by two before His face" (Luke 10:1 NKJV). These two men would have been included in the seventy, but they likely missed out because they delayed their obedience from a lack of godly fear.

In my years of ministering to God's people, it still causes me to marvel (in the wrong way) when I hear a believer nonchalantly comment, "God has been dealing with me about this matter for a couple months." They smile and sometimes even laugh it off, as if it's a cute thing. If only they realized they were bragging about their lack of holy fear, I don't think they'd take it so lightly.

What if Moses delayed turning aside from his busy activities of tending the flocks to see the great sight of the burning bush (Exodus 3)?

What if Noah delayed building the ark?

What if Abram delayed going to Canaan? His dad did, for he was the first one called to go to Canaan. What his dad missed in his delay, Abram fulfilled (Genesis 11:31).

What if Nehemiah delayed finishing the wall to satisfy the request of Sanballat and Geshem, the two leaders, to halt the work and travel to meet with them? But Nehemiah feared God. His response was, "I am engaged in a great work, so I can't come. Why should I stop working to come and meet with you?" (Nehemiah 6:3).

The examples are endless. The bottom line is this: when we tremble at His Word, we obey God immediately.

Making It Personal

Passage: "I will honor those who honor me, and I will *despise* those who *think lightly* of me." (1 Samuel 2:30)

Point: If we delay our obedience to God's Word for personal excuses, we communicate that His will is secondary in importance.

Ponder: It's possible that seemingly harmless things can detour us from fulfilling God's will. When what is not sin takes precedence over the Word of the Lord, it becomes sin. Have I allowed myself to be distracted by personal interests and therefore delayed my obedience? How can this change?

Prayer: Dear heavenly Father, forgive me for the times I've treated Your Word as optional or not prioritized it as most important. I realize in doing so I've inadvertently communicated what is important to You to be trivial to me. I repent and ask Your forgiveness. I will give top priority to what You desire. In Jesus' name I pray, amen.

Profession: Once I know the will of God, I will immediately obey it.

We're not called to live by human reason. All that matters is obedience to God's Word and His leading in our lives. When we are in His will, we are in the safest place in the world.

—BROTHER YUN

24 | IT MAKES NO SENSE

In the past, has the Holy Spirit led you to do something that didn't make sense? Most who've walked closely with God for any length of time would answer yes. But let me ask another question: Did it make sense after you obeyed—sometimes immediately, or even a while later? Almost always, yes. (I say "almost always" because there are *rare* occasions when it may not make sense until we arrive at the judgment seat.) Continuing to examine what it means to tremble at God's Word, one who truly walks in holy fear will:

1. Obey God immediately.
2. **Obey God even if it doesn't make sense.**

It's not a common occurrence that God asks us to do something that doesn't make sense to our understanding. But it does happen. Let's ask questions.

Did it make sense to spit into the dirt and put the mud on a blind man's eyes and then tell him to go wash it off? No, it didn't at the time, but this counsel (wisdom) gave a blind man sight.

Did it make sense to pour water into wine containers in the middle of a wedding when what was needed was more wine? No, it didn't at the time, but this counsel (wisdom) resulted in the finest wine of the wedding.

Did it make sense to instruct experienced sailors to go against their instinct and training, to not abandon a sinking ship when lifeboats were readily available? No, it didn't at the time, but this counsel (wisdom) saved all 276 men on board; not one life was lost (Acts 27:27–36).

Did it make sense for a man to leave a citywide revival meeting, one that God used him to initiate, and obey the command to go out in the middle of the desert? No, it didn't at the time, but this counsel (wisdom) made way for the third in command of Ethiopia to be saved.

Did it make sense to walk around towering and fortified walls of a large city quietly for six days, then on the seventh day, to do the same seven more times, and finally blow horns and shout? No, it didn't at the time, but this counsel (wisdom) saw the enemy's walls come crashing down.

Did it make sense to put flour into a pot of poisonous stew and then tell all the ministers to eat it? No, it didn't at the time, but this counsel (wisdom) gave everyone a nourishing meal, and nobody got sick.

Does it make sense to forgive those who have hurt you, your family, or someone close to you? Shouldn't they pay?

Does it make sense to love those who hate you? Shouldn't they be given the cold shoulder?

Does it make sense to do good to those who have mistreated you? Shouldn't you get even with them?

Does it make sense to honor those in authority who are acting wickedly? Shouldn't we be complaining and rebelling?

Does it make sense to honor those who treat you dishonorably? Shouldn't they be told off?

I could continue for the rest of the chapter, and possibly the entire book, sharing commands that don't make sense in Scripture, but based on the results, every one of them proved to be the wisdom of God. Those involved either trembled at God's instructions, obeyed, and were blessed; or they lacked godly fear in their neglect or disobedience and suffered the consequences. I hope you are seeing with more clarity how the fear of the Lord truly is the beginning of wisdom (Psalm 111:10). We are told:

Trust in the Lord with all your heart; *do not depend* on your own understanding. Seek his will in all you do, and he will show you which path to take. (Proverbs 3:5–6)

The Lord's wisdom far exceeds our own; therefore, we shouldn't depend on our own understanding. We can easily be swayed from obedience that will ultimately benefit us when we are instructed to do something that's not logical. The person who fears God obeys, even when it doesn't make sense.

A few years back I met with a multibillionaire. He shared of his floundering work in the marketplace early in his career. He had read all the bestsellers regarding building a successful business and implemented the wisdom he gleaned. Yet he still struggled.

One day while sitting in church listening to his pastor bring a message, the thought came to him, *He is called to preach the gospel and depends on the Holy Spirit to accomplish his life mission. I'm called to the marketplace, so why don't I depend on the Holy Spirit to do what I'm called to?*

He determined to get up each morning and ask the Lord's direction for the day. He kept a notepad and wrote down everything he was impressed to do. He also made it a point to keep one ear always listening to the Holy Spirit's impressions throughout the day, even in his business meetings.

He shared some specifics. On a particular day he was scheduled for an acquisitions meeting. That morning he felt the Holy Spirit instruct him to do what seemed like a very trivial act. It made no sense, but he was committed to the process.

The Holy Spirit instructed him to repetitively commit a certain act. He kept thinking of the king who was told by the prophet Elisha to strike the ground with arrows. The king struck three times and was rebuked by the prophet for not striking more (2 Kings 13:14–19). So this man performed the act twenty times. He told me later, "That day my company bought twenty hospitals in Vietnam."

Then he shared how he bought one of the largest banks in the world in Europe. The process seemed more unorthodox than the hospital acquisitions. I was amazed. Simply put, this businessman chose to obey God no matter what was given to him in prayer, whether it seemed logical or not. The fruit is evident—he's not floundering any longer!

When one of our sons was in his late teenage years, I asked him to do something that didn't make sense to him. He stood toe-to-toe with me protesting that my instruction didn't add up, but I stood firm. In exasperation, he finally said, "Dad, I'm a millennial, and we need to understand the 'why' before we do something!"

I said to him, "Okay, I'll make you a deal. Let me set it up by telling you a true story. God told a young prophet of Judah to travel to Bethel, prophesy to the king of Israel, and not return to Judah by the same route he came, and furthermore, to not eat anything on the entire trip. The young prophet did not obey the instructions of the Holy Spirit and suffered the consequences; he was killed by a lion before the trip was over" (1 Kings 13:16, 23–26). "Son, here's my deal with you. The day you can give me the 'why' behind those specific instructions to the young prophet is the day I will tell you the 'why' behind my instructions."

To this day, he has not been able to tell me the "why." In fact, that one also puzzles me. There are times God will tell us to do something that just doesn't make sense in our minds. But His wisdom is always confirmed by the results. This is why Jesus states, "Wisdom is shown to be right by its results" (Matthew 11:19).

May we all be like Peter who, after toiling at sea all night with nothing to show for it, heeded Jesus' voice to launch back out to deeper waters and cast his nets once again. That command would take a lot of extra work when they were already exhausted. Don't you love Peter's response? "We worked hard all last night and didn't catch a thing. But if you say so, I'll let the nets down again" (Luke 5:5). The result was two boatloads of fish.

Making It Personal

Passage: Those who trust their own insight are foolish, but anyone who walks in wisdom is safe. (Proverbs 28:26)

Point: The Lord's wisdom far exceeds ours; therefore, we shouldn't depend on our own understanding. It can easily sway us from beneficial obedience. The person who fears God obeys, even when it doesn't make sense.

Ponder: Do I have trouble trusting God's wisdom? In the past, have I second-guessed His counsel and fallen back on what seemed logical to me? How did that work out? What would happen if I looked to God for direction and trusted Him? Can I commit to this process?

Prayer: Dear heavenly Father, forgive me for trusting in my own wisdom over Yours. I ask for faith to receive Your wisdom as I read Your Word, pray, and hear godly counsel from those who fear You. Give me the strength to believe and obey even if it doesn't make sense. In Jesus' name I pray, amen.

Profession: I choose to obey God's wisdom over my own and the voices of those who trust in mankind's ability over God's.

*It is man's duty to love
and to fear God, even
without hope of reward
or fear of punishment.*

—MAIMONIDES

25 | NO OBVIOUS BENEFIT

You've probably heard a parent bemoan the fact that the only time they hear from their son or daughter attending university is when they need money. In this typical scenario, during that rare phone call the child might sound interested in conversing with mom and dad, but the underlying motive is the benefit of the needed resource. Holy fear protects us from doing this with our heavenly Father and introduces our next aspect of trembling at God's Word. Let's review as we add our newest indicator. We are to

1. Obey God immediately.
2. Obey God even if it doesn't make sense.
3. **Obey God even when you don't see a personal benefit.**

In over forty years of ministry, I've observed a sad reality, especially in the Western church. All too often, to get believers interested in obedience, benefits must be emphasized. Think about it. Would we come thirty minutes early for a front-row seat to hear a message on holiness? Are book titles that emphasize obedience making the bestseller lists? Has leadership strayed from confrontational truth to accommodate this trend? In other words, have numerous ministers succumbed to the pressure of gratifying itching ears with inspiring stories, rather than calling God's people to deny themselves to follow Jesus?

What makes this trend such a sad reality? In shunning God's wisdom, we actually hurt ourselves. His commands, counsel, and wisdom ultimately bring the greatest blessings, both in this life and the one to come. We are told there is "a great reward for those who obey" God's Word (Psalm 19:11). You can never outgive God; the benefits are far greater than anything you can do for Him.

On the other hand, it's dangerous to be motivated by incentives. Why? If the benefit isn't obvious, will we have the same resolve to obey God's instructions? Most likely it will be swallowed up by personal interests. This is why the fear of the Lord is so crucial; it motivates obedience, whether a reward is obvious or not.

During the time of the great Persian Empire, this mighty kingdom had subdued all others, and their leader, King Xerxes, was the most powerful man on earth. He was married to a Jewish woman named Esther.

The highest-ranking official under the king was a man named Haman. He was bitterly offended by Esther's cousin Mordecai, also an official to the king. In his rage, Haman determined to punish not only Mordecai but also the entire race of Jewish people. He, as well as most others, was unaware Queen Esther was Jewish.

Haman proceeded to viciously slander the Jewish people to the king and suggest the entire race be annihilated in one day. His plot was successful. The king consented, issued the decree, and sealed it with his signet ring.

Mordecai, in discovering the news of the decree, sent a messenger to his cousin, Queen Esther. He asked her to go to the king and plea for the lives of the Jewish people.

Esther replied, "All the king's officials and even the people in the provinces know that anyone who appears before the king in his inner court without being invited is doomed to die unless the king holds out his gold scepter. And the king has not called for me to come to him" (Esther 4:11).

Even though Esther was Xerxes' wife, if she were to approach him in the throne room without being invited, most likely she would be executed.

Let's think this through: She is queen; she has a fabulous life—in fact, anything her heart desires. She personally has nothing to gain by the risk of entering the throne room for the sake of God's people, but she has everything to lose, including her head. Yet notice to her response to Mordecai:

> "Go and gather together all the Jews of Susa and fast for me. Do not eat or drink for three days, night or day. My maids and I will do the same. And then, though it is against the law, I *will go* in to see the king. *If I must die, I must die.*" (Esther 4:15–16)

Holy fear motivated her to put God's kingdom before her own welfare. Her comfort, security, wealth, and position were all put in jeopardy by her obedience. There was nothing in it for her, yet what was important to God was most important to her, no exceptions. She trembled at His Word; she feared God.

In 2015, Lisa and I were in Yerevan, Armenia, ministering at a conference to 3,500 leaders. Pastors had flown in from all over Eastern Europe and the Middle East, and many had driven from Iran (Yerevan is thirty miles from Iran's border). At that time, the Iranian citizens were permitted to enter Armenia, so numerous leaders from the underground church were in attendance. The meetings were glorious.

After the final meeting concluded, Lisa and I decided to stroll down the main street of Yerevan to get some fresh air. Two young ladies in their midtwenties ran out of a restaurant to greet us. It turns out they were two leaders from Iran. They were stunningly beautiful and full of life; in fact, at one point I thought, *Which two of my three single sons can I introduce these girls to?*

Lisa and I talked with them for about twenty minutes. We learned the religious police were tracking them; during the conference, calls were made from the Iranian authorities concerning their whereabouts. One of the young ladies shared she had an alarming message on her phone.

At that point I uttered one of the stupidest comments I've made in four decades of ministry. I said to her, "Why are you going back? Why don't you defect?"

She sincerely, kindly, and with resolve looked at me and answered, "Who will tell the Persian people about Jesus if we don't go back?"

I was in awe of her response. We witnessed these ladies laying aside the instinct to protect themselves; it was overshadowed by their passion for the advancement of the kingdom in their nation. They walked in the same holy fear Esther did. They obeyed God, even when no personal benefit was obvious, and quite possibly, they put their lives in danger. I was both corrected and inspired.

This resolve, as seen in these young ladies, isn't isolated to a single act of obedience. It's a heart posture that is developed and lived by. It is our default in even the seemingly insignificant decisions we make moment by moment. We choose, even in the small matters, to obey God's Word and the Holy Spirit's leading. We may have a busy schedule but suddenly are prompted to call someone. There's no reason, no obvious benefit, but we aren't motivated by this. We make the call, and often we see the "why" later.

Or perhaps we learn that someone slandered us. There's no obvious benefit to forgive, seek reconciliation, and bless this person, but we choose to do so strictly out of obedience to the command to "[forgive] one another, even as God in Christ forgave you" and to "bless those who curse you" (Ephesians 4:32; Luke 6:28 NKJV).

Perhaps we've been mistreated by someone who hates us. What is the noticeable benefit of obeying Jesus' words to "do good to those who hate you, and pray for those who spitefully use you" (Matthew 5:44 NKJV)? Or consider this: What benefit do believers in persecuted nations see in blessing those who persecute them, torture them, or even put their loved ones to death for their faith? Yet Lisa and I have sat with pastors in nations where this has happened and witnessed their abundant joy and life.

What benefit is there in praying passionately for those in other nations? Or giving to those in other nations who will never be able to repay you? The list is endless. The question is, will you consistently obey God in response to the holy fear that burns in your heart, or will you wait until you see a personal benefit?

═════ Making It Personal ═════

Passage: "If you try to *hang on to your life*, you will lose it. But if you give up your life for my sake, you will save it." (Matthew 16:25)

Point: We most often miss the greatest blessings by shunning God's wisdom that doesn't appear to be personally beneficial. In essence, we hurt ourselves in the long run. We can never outgive God.

Ponder: What does Jesus mean in saying, "Hang on to your life"? Have I looked at this scripture in light of only the extreme cases, such as martyrdom? Have I applied it to the small, everyday decisions I make? What would happen if I did? How would this change the way I live?

Prayer: Dear heavenly Father, forgive me for limiting my hunger and obedience to the wisdom that I deem personally beneficial. I repent of this mindset and ask Your forgiveness. I choose from this moment forward to no longer hang on to my life but to give it up for Jesus' sake. Therefore, I will hunger and thirst for Your wisdom, even that which doesn't carry an immediate benefit. In Jesus' name I pray, amen.

Profession: I choose, moment by moment, to give my life for the desires and wisdom of my Lord Jesus.

Apart from obedience, there can be no salvation, for salvation without obedience is a self-contradictory impossibility.

—A.W. TOZER

26 | A GOOD PAIN

When a woman gives birth to her child it is not a pleasant experience; it's difficult and even painful. However, the end result is a desired new family member. Without the discomfort of the pregnancy and delivery, this beautiful new life couldn't have been brought forth. This offers a glimpse into the next aspect of trembling at God's Word. The first three indicators, along with the newest, are to

1. Obey God immediately.
2. Obey God even if it doesn't make sense.
3. Obey God even when you don't see a personal benefit.
4. **Obey God even if it is painful.**

Going back to one of our foundational scriptures, Philippians 2:12–13, we are reminded to work out our salvation with fear and trembling. Just prior to these words calling for our *obedience*, Paul points to Jesus as setting the example. Our Lord relinquished His divine privileges and "humbled himself in *obedience* to God and died a criminal's death on a cross" (Philippians 2:8). Jesus willingly obeyed the Father's request even though it would necessitate tremendous suffering.

The night before the crucifixion, in the garden of Gethsemane, Jesus cried out in anguish, "My Father! If it is possible, let this cup of suffering be taken away from me. Yet I want your will to be done, not mine" (Matthew 26:39). The conflict between obedience and self-preservation was so intense that Jesus sweat great drops of blood. Remember, He "faced all of the same testings we do, yet he did not sin" (Hebrews 4:15). He foresaw the horrific suffering ahead and pleaded for an alternate path to accomplish the Father's will, but it wasn't possible. What motivates this degree of obedience?

> While Jesus was here on earth, he offered prayers and pleadings, with a loud cry and tears . . . And God heard his prayers because of *his deep reverence for God.* (Hebrews 5:7)

His deep holy fear empowered Him to face and endure what human nature would run from. In the same way, we are told:

> Since Christ suffered for us in the flesh, *arm yourselves* also with the same mind, for he who has suffered in the flesh has ceased from sin. (1 Peter 4:1 NKJV)

Before going any further, allow me to interject an important point. False religion will seek out suffering for the sake of pleasing the god it serves. True Christianity seeks to obey God and, in the process, faces a fallen world's resistance, which often results in suffering. Obedience is what pleases God, not seeking out hardship. Suffering can occur physically or mentally; the pain of either is very real.

Peter instructs us to *arm ourselves.* Can you imagine a military going to war without any planes, ships, tanks, guns, bullets, knives—unarmed? Just the thought of it seems ludicrous. In the same way, it's just as crazy for a believer to be unprepared to suffer, yet many are. An unarmed believer can easily bypass hardship for the sake of self-preservation. The fear of the Lord is what arms us; it maintains a deep resolve in our will to obey God no matter what suffering it may entail.

There are numerous stories I could share about suffering, enough to fill an entire book. One story relates to a ministry trip in the early 1990s.

Lisa, our children, and I were in a very small town in the middle of nowhere ministering for a church that had just lost its pastor; he had left them for a larger church.

The first few meetings were rough; a good part of the congregation was disinterested, and the young people sat in the back joking and laughing. However, by the third meeting a breakthrough occurred. The impact was profound; even the young people were now coming early to grab the front-row seats. The attendance grew, and the meetings extended for a few weeks. We met every evening in a packed small church building, with several saved and most everyone revived.

After a lot of prayer, we offered to stay for however many months it would take to prepare the church for a new pastor. However, the board wasn't happy with the disruption to their calculated lives and control over the way things ran. Shockingly, one of their complaints was that they didn't appreciate the young people taking their seats in the front row. There were other gripes, but nothing worth listing. In short, they eventually voted not to accept our offer and for us to leave.

The same evening of their vote, I announced to the church our final meeting would be the next night. An outcry of disappointment came from most of the people; it was an intense, disconcerting, and uncomfortable moment.

The next day the church received a call from a disgruntled man whose wife had been attending the meetings, and he threatened to bomb the church building during our last meeting. I laughed about it, until a police-man phoned me about the matter.

In disbelief I retorted, "Surely this won't happen."

The officer answered, "Sir, I know this man. He's a suspected high-level drug runner, and I wouldn't put it past him to do it if he has a few drinks."

Concerned, I asked, "Can't you give us some protection?"

I could hardly believe his reply: "My station, which is the nearest one to this small town, is thirty-five miles away. I get off tonight at 6 p.m., and no one else can drive over because we are understaffed."

I hung up the phone in disbelief, but even more so, I was greatly concerned. My mind was screaming to immediately pack up our things and leave town. We were living in a member's double-wide trailer parked in a field, completely vulnerable to attack. We felt unsafe and rejected. Why even go that evening? The board spurned us; we should just leave town!

I knew my thoughts were selfish; there were many people impacted during our couple of weeks of ministry, and if we abandoned them prematurely over a threat, they would again experience the rejection of a leader. I knew if we ran, we would set a pattern of compromise that could possibly affect us the rest of our lives. I couldn't help but think of Jesus' words: "The hired servant (*he who merely serves for wages*) . . . when he sees the wolf coming, deserts the flock and runs away" (John 10:12 AMPC).

We prayed for hours. Repeatedly, I heard in my heart the scripture that states those who abide in God's presence are those who "keep their promises even when it hurts" (Psalm 15:4). Finally, a peace prevailed in our hearts, and we felt it would be safe. We had a great service that evening. No bomb was set off, and we were able to properly say good-bye to the congregation.

We live in a fallen world that is contrary, and even hostile, to God's ways. This is why we are informed, "It has been granted on behalf of Christ, not only to believe in Him, but also to suffer for His sake" (Philippians 1:29 NKJV). Not only Paul, but Peter also writes,

> For God called you to do good, even if it means suffering, just as Christ suffered for you. He is your example, and you must follow in his steps. He never sinned, nor deceived anyone. He did not retaliate when he was insulted, nor threaten revenge when he suffered. He left his case in the hands of God, who always judges fairly. (1 Peter 2:21–23)

We are not to retaliate; rather, we are to commit any unjust treatment we receive into the hands of God. We shouldn't ignore it, but in prayer we should turn it over to Him. God will avenge us, but in His way and time frame.

The heroes of the kingdom experienced great victories through their faith, but in their obedience to God, some were mocked, chained, tortured, abused, imprisoned, wandered in deserts, lived in caves, and myriad other uncomfortable or painful circumstances. Why? They lived in a fallen world that is hostile to the kingdom of God (Hebrews 11:36–39). They all had this in common: Out of their holy fear they refused to turn away from obedience, even if it hurt. But they were confident in this promise, "Those who plant in tears will harvest with shouts of joy . . . they sing as they return with the harvest" (Psalm 126:5–6).

Making It Personal

Passage: In the fear of the LORD there is strong confidence, and His children will have a place of refuge. (Proverbs 14:26 NKJV)

Point: The fear of the Lord is what arms us to maintain a deep resolve to obey God, even in the face of adversity.

Ponder: Have I bypassed obedience to God's Word for the sake of self-preservation? Am I willing to repent and embrace the fear of the Lord? Will I choose to love and obey even if it costs me financially, socially, or even physically?

Prayer: Dear Lord, forgive me for the pattern of avoiding obedience to Your Word in order to protect myself. I realize I've chosen unwisely— Your protection is infallible and enduring; my protection is only temporary. From this moment forward I choose the fear of the Lord; may it give me the deep resolve to obey You no matter the cost. Thank You for this strength, in Jesus' name, amen.

Profession: I am armed by holy fear to obey God even if it means I will suffer in the process. I commit my soul to Him who judges fairly.

*Mark out a straight
path for your feet; stay
on the safe path.*

—PROVERBS 4:26

27 | IT IS FINISHED

To begin this chapter, let me ask a question: Is it possible to reach the full potential of any project without completing it? The answer is an obvious no. Our Lord has a massive project in process, which centers on building a kingdom. He has given each of us the responsibility of subprojects, which when completed will finish the work of His glorious kingdom.

Keep this truth in mind as we transition into our final aspect of trembling at God's Word. Here again are the first four, along with the last:

1. Obey God immediately.
2. Obey God even if it doesn't make sense.
3. Obey God even when you don't see a personal benefit.
4. Obey God even if it is painful.
5. **Obey God to completion.**

The first king of Israel, Saul, is a classic example of someone who doesn't tremble at God's Word. He easily strayed from obedience when it didn't make sense, the benefit wasn't obvious, or it didn't serve his purposes. His lack of holy fear frequently caused pain or harm to others, which is the case with all such behavior.

This wasn't always the case. Before being crowned king, he was a humble and God-fearing young man—two virtues that go hand in hand.

165

When Samuel, the renowned prophet, sought him out, he was quick to say, "Why would you notice me? I'm from the smallest tribe of Israel, and my family is the least important in our tribe" (1 Samuel 9:21, author's paraphrase). Later, all of Israel had gathered to discover the identity of their first king. After a lengthy process, the divine selection fell to Saul, but when the leaders called for him, he was not to be found; he was hiding in an obscure place. He had no desire to be recognized (1 Samuel 10:20–24).

Holy fear would not prove to be his treasure. As with Solomon, he eventually forsook it once he experienced success, notoriety, and the benefits of leadership. As with most, including King Saul, the initial signs of losing holy fear are subtle. It begins with ignoring conviction in the small matters, resulting in our consciences becoming more and more desensitized. Eventually, when faced with the more significant matters, we're unaware of our developed pattern of disobedience.

This was true of King Saul. Signs of losing holy fear began to surface (1 Samuel 13:5–14), but what made it tricky is that he was experiencing great success at the same time (1 Samuel 14:47).

After a while, the king was commanded to "go and completely destroy the entire Amalekite nation—men, women, children, babies, cattle, sheep, goats, camels, and donkeys" (1 Samuel 15:3). The Lord was ready to avenge this nation's wicked behavior.

Saul mobilized 210,000 troops. He and his men slaughtered every human being and domestic animal—except for the Amalekite king, Agag, and the finest domestic animals (1 Samuel 15:7–9).

Let's think this through. For Saul to commission this large of an army, the Amalekites would have had at least a quarter of a million citizens, so in essence, they butchered 249,999 people. The king accomplished 99.99 percent of what he was told to do, but notice God's response to his *almost* complete obedience:

> "I am sorry that I ever made Saul king, for he has not been loyal to me and has *refused to obey* my command." (1 Samuel 15:11)

Samuel relays this message to the king and bluntly calls his behavior *rebellion* (1 Samuel 15:23). There is no doubt about it, Saul *sinned*. Let's pause briefly and discuss sin. The apostle John says that sin is lawlessness (1 John 3:4). His definition of sin can be stated as such: *sin is insubordination to the authority of God*. Look at it from this angle: In the garden, Adam didn't jump in bed with a prostitute, rob a bank, or murder someone. He simply disobeyed what God said. In the same manner, Saul chose to not *fully* obey what God instructed him to do.

Let's dive deeper. When Saul was asked to go to battle, he didn't stomp his foot and say, "No way! I'm not going to do this!" Most would classify that behavior as rebellion. He didn't ignore the command and busy himself with other personal matters. If that were the case, most would conclude, "He erred in judgment by not making obedience a priority." But few would use the word "rebellion."

Likewise, most would affirm he did well by completing 99.99 percent of the assignment, but very few would classify his actions as rebellion. If we were in Saul's shoes and received this correction, how many of us would protest, "Come on, be reasonable! Why are you so focused on the little I didn't do, instead of acknowledging all that I accomplished?" In light of this, it's safe to conclude this truth: *almost complete* obedience isn't obedience at all.

Let's explore why such strong words were used. First, in those days, if you were a king who conquered another nation, to take their king alive was akin to having a living trophy in your palace. It served as a constant reminder of the greatness of your leadership, not only for your ego but for all who entered your palace.

Second, why spare the best animals? Before answering, let's complicate it even further. Saul allowed the very best domestic animals to be spared for the purpose of gifting them to the Lord. Note his rebuttal to the prophet: "'It's true that the army spared the best of the sheep, goats, and cattle,' Saul admitted. 'But they are going to sacrifice them to the LORD your God. We have destroyed everything else'" (1 Samuel 15:15). Why would he do this? Might this have been done to secure favor with his people? This is a nation that acknowledges the Lord God. Think of the soldiers', priests', and people's perspective; they most likely were saying to one another, "We have such a godly king; he always puts the Lord first; he's giving the very best to God." The people didn't know the original command was to destroy absolutely everything. In essence, Saul was securing his reputation. The motivation behind his actions was the fear of man. Saul was insecure.

In our world today, many are empathetic toward those who are insecure. However, what's behind insecurity is our desire to be accepted, loved, or respected, even at the price of disobedience. We lack the realization of how deeply accepted and loved we are by our Creator. Insecurity needs to be called out for what it is: a dangerous trap.

Saul didn't complete the command due to his lack of holy fear. Let's return to Jesus' example. He was facing rejection, shame, hatred, grueling opposition, physical beatings, and horrific crucifixion. When the temple guard came for the arrest, His disciples tried to prevent it and protect Jesus; however, His response was,

> "Don't you realize that I could ask my Father for thousands of angels to protect us, and he would send them instantly? But if I did, how would the Scriptures be fulfilled that describe what must happen now?" (Matthew 26:53–54)

Obedience to completion was paramount to Jesus.

In high school, I wasn't a believer, but there was a poster in our locker room that riveted me. I'd see it every afternoon after basketball practice. It had an athlete sitting with his head hung low saying, "I quit." Below that image was a picture of Jesus hanging on the cross saying, "I didn't quit."

That left an indelible impression on me as an unbeliever. Now that I understand that Jesus could have avoided the gruesome treatment and brutal death but rather chose to continue in obedience until He could finally say, "It is finished," it carries much more weight. He set the example for us to fully obey—to finish whatever God entrusts to us.

Now we can better understand His instructions to the disciples when they cried out for their faith to be increased:

"When you have done *all those things* which you are commanded, say, 'We are unprofitable servants. We have done what was our duty to do.'" (Luke 17:10 NKJV)

His words "all those things" take on a whole new meaning. Let's always obey to completion.

══════════ Making It Personal ══════════

Passage: Never quit! . . . Keep your eyes on *Jesus*, who both began and finished this race we're in. Study how he did it. Because he never lost sight of where he was headed—that exhilarating finish in and with God—he could put up with anything along the way . . . When you find yourselves flagging in your faith, go over that story again, item by item, that long litany of hostility he plowed through. *That* will shoot adrenaline into your souls! (Hebrews 12:2–3 MSG)

Point: *Almost* complete obedience isn't obedience at all. Jesus set the example for us to fully obey—to the finish—whatever God entrusts to us.

Ponder: Have I started to obey God's Word and allowed distractions, pleasure, resistance, disapproval of others, or any other adversity to cause me to cease and not finish? How can this change?

Prayer: Dear heavenly Father, please forgive me for starting to obey what You've told me to do but not finishing, either by ignoring it or changing my mind because of not seeing it as self-serving. I repent of this lack of holy fear and ask Your forgiveness. In Jesus' name I pray, amen.

Profession: I choose to obey God's Word to completion.

When men no longer fear God, they transgress His laws without hesitation. The fear of consequences is no deterrent when the fear of God is gone.

—A.W. TOZER

28 | HOW TO SEAR A CONSCIENCE

As stated in the previous chapter, the initial signs of losing holy fear are subtle—so subtle that we need to focus in a little more and elaborate on this important point. Have you ever experienced a gut warning when presented with an opportunity to do something questionable? Most understand it's our *conscience* safeguarding us, but what many don't realize is that the clarity and strength of our conscience can be altered.

Our conscience is a gift from God that should never be taken lightly. It's an integral part of our *heart*; its sensitivity is strengthened by holy fear and, conversely, dulled by the lack thereof. We are warned: "Guard your *heart* above all else, for it determines the course of your life" (Proverbs 4:23).

When I was in my early thirties, a well-known minister asked me to lunch. During the course of our meal, he asked, "John, how do I keep from falling like so many other leaders have?"

I almost choked on my food. Why would he pose such a question to me? I was young, and he'd been in ministry longer than I'd been saved. But rather than defer, I looked inside and silently asked, *Holy Spirit, what answer do I give him?*

Almost instantly I heard, *Tell him to guard his conscience as his most prized possession.*

I spoke what I heard, then suddenly, words came pouring out of my soul along these lines: "You will be offered great opportunities, but inside you will know it violates integrity, is not above board, is questionable, or could hurt others. Listen to your conscience; don't shun its warning. If you ignore it, you'll forfeit your sensitivity to God."

In the ensuing days I discovered "conscience" appears frequently in Scripture, something I hadn't previously been aware of. It's found approximately thirty times in the New Testament alone. Paul writes to Timothy:

> Cling to your faith in Christ, and keep your *conscience* clear. For some people have deliberately violated their *consciences*; as a result, their faith has been shipwrecked. (1 Timothy 1:19)

Shipwrecked faith is not a trivial matter.

The lunch with the older minister opened my eyes to the weight of Paul's statement. It confirmed why many don't finish well.

For Scripture to admonish us to "keep" our conscience clear means initially it's in good condition. The blood of Jesus cleanses and purifies our conscience (1 Timothy 3:9; Hebrews 9:9, 14). This is one of the great benefits of the new birth. Jeremiah the prophet makes a statement regarding our conscience that is often misapplied. He declares, "The heart is deceitful above all things, and desperately wicked; who can know it?" (17:9 NKJV). He is not speaking of those who have been born again, with a new nature, recreated in the likeness of Jesus. The Old Testament people didn't have a new heart. But God promised them, "I will give you a new heart and put a new spirit within you" (Ezekiel 36:26 NKJV). It would happen when Jesus redeemed our nature and gave us His.

Due to the miracle of becoming a brand-new person in Christ, we have a trustworthy conscience. The challenge is keeping it pure. So now we must ask, how do we defile it? The full corruption doesn't happen in a moment;

rather, most of the time it starts with smaller matters and eventually, if not addressed, ends in a shipwreck. James writes:

> But don't just listen to God's word. You must *do what it says*. Otherwise, you are only fooling yourselves. (James 1:22)

We come face-to-face again with the concept of obedience. We've thoroughly discussed the evidence of holy fear being immediate and full obedience—even if it doesn't make sense, a benefit isn't evident, or it hurts. The person who walks accordingly cannot fool themselves.

Let's pause and make sure the impact isn't missed. It's certainly possible to fool acquaintances—even close friends and family—but it is another matter to fool ourselves. In essence, when we disobey, we *deceive ourselves*. We weaken truth's protection, and our sense of moral navigation is compromised. We're less aware of being in harm's way.

Let's give a hypothetical example of the process. Have you ever spoken a slanderous word against someone? The moment you did, perhaps it felt like a knife had been thrust into your gut; that's your conscience's voice. Hopefully you listened, repented, and immediately corrected what you spoke. However, what happens so often is we justify our behavior. The ensuing reasoning might sound something like, *What I spoke is accurate!* Sadly, our misguided argument prevails, and we stick to our statement while ignoring the inner caution. We've now begun the defiling process; our conscience's sensitivity is weakened.

The next time we speak out against someone, it's not a knife hitting our gut; now we feel a hard pinch in our inward parts. Our conscience has spoken again, but this time with a less recognizable voice. Now the internal conflict is not as intense; it's easier to ignore the warning and justify our words. Yet we've further polluted our heart, and our conscience's sensitivity diminishes even more.

When we speak out against someone again, we don't sense a hard pinch; now it's merely a tingle—barely recognizable. We hardly need to convince ourselves with reasoning because our conscience's voice is so soft. It's easier to justify our behavior. Our conscience's sensitivity diminishes yet again.

Finally, we don't feel anything at all. Our conscience has been seared. We are past feeling blinded and have forfeited all sense of discernment. Now we are without any moral navigation, and our faith's shipwreck is imminent. In essence, we've fooled ourselves—we're self-deceived.

All of this could have been averted through simple repentance—a complete change of mind and heart. It's when we acknowledge our wisdom is futile and we firmly embrace the wisdom of God. "He who covers his sins will not prosper, but whoever confesses and forsakes them will have mercy" (Proverbs 28:13 NKJV).

Mercy and restoration can happen at any stage of the process, but the lack of holy fear delays our response. We gamble because our heart becomes more and more desensitized to the conviction of our conscience. The wise person is always quick to respond with repentance to his or her conscience's warnings; they know that to delay is dangerous.

There are many, both in Scripture and in our day, who've delayed listening to their conscience. It can be compared to playing Russian roulette. You might escape shipwreck, but how do you know when you've gone past feeling? There's no voice that warns, "If you ignore me one more time, I will be silenced." Paul laments:

> Now the Spirit expressly says that in latter times some will depart from the faith, giving heed to deceiving spirits and doctrines of demons, speaking lies in hypocrisy, having their own *conscience seared* with a hot iron. (1 Timothy 4:1–2 NKJV)

Human skin seared with a hot iron loses all feeling. The same is true with our conscience. Now we project ourselves contrary to who we actually are without any conviction. This is what happened with Ananias, Sapphira, King Saul, and many others.

The other consequence of searing is that it locks things in. If you sear meat, it keeps the juices from escaping. Paul writes, "I am not lying, my *conscience* also bearing me witness in the Holy Spirit" (Romans 9:1 NKJV). If a believer has seared their conscience, then they can no longer communicate with the Holy Spirit. His witness cannot reach our soul, no different from the juices that can't escape the meat. They now are without life's navigation system. Their path is one of destruction.

In closing, listen to a couple of Paul's many statements: "Brothers, I have always lived before God with a clear conscience!" (Acts 23:1). Again, "I always try to maintain a clear conscience before God and all people" (Acts 24:16). In conclusion, let's guard our hearts diligently.

Making It Personal

Passage: Let us go right into the presence of God with sincere hearts fully trusting him. For our guilty consciences have been sprinkled with Christ's blood to make us clean. (Hebrews 10:22)

Point: The clarity and strength of our conscience can be altered. Our sensitivity is strengthened by holy fear and, conversely, is dulled by the lack thereof.

Ponder: Our consciences are made pure by the blood of Jesus Christ. What spiritual discipline can I put in place to keep my conscience clear?

Prayer: Dear heavenly Father, I ask forgiveness for the times I've ignored and gone against my conscience. I'm sorry for not diligently guarding it. I repent and ask Your forgiveness. Please cleanse me with the blood of Jesus. Restore a pure conscience within me, one that is tender and sensitive to Your voice and leading. May I be quick to obey You in all things. In Jesus' name, amen.

Profession: I will guard my heart diligently and be sensitive to the leading and voice of my conscience.

Intimacy
With
God

WEEK 5

I would rather pay the price to hear God's voice personally, regardless of how difficult the circumstances may be, than to have to settle for always hearing from Him secondhand.

—JOY DAWSON

29 | WHERE INTIMACY BEGINS

As holy fear grows within us according to our increased comprehension of God's glory, it purifies our motives, frees us from the fear of man, and produces true holiness in our lives. The manifestation of holy fear is immediate and complete obedience to God regardless of whether we see a reason or benefit or how painful it is.

With this knowledge, we can now turn our discussion to this unique gift's benefits, and in this section we'll focus on what is undoubtably the greatest benefit of all: intimacy with God.

The word *intimate* comes from two Latin words: *intus*, which means "within," and *intimus*, which means "very secret."[1] In joining the two, we come up with "innermost secrets." This gives a very good picture of *intimacy*, a word used to describe an affectionate connection between two close friends on levels far deeper than merely an acquaintance, which is someone you've met and know slightly but not well.

To be intimate is a two-way street; both parties need to know each other's innermost desires and thoughts. Regarding intimacy with God, let's look at both His and our perspectives, starting with His. David writes:

> O LORD, you have *examined* my heart and *know* everything about me.
> (Psalm 139:1)

The word *examined* is the Hebrew word *ḥāqar*, which is defined "to explore, to search, to seek out." This perfectly describes what it takes to enter into an intimate relationship with someone. Time and effort, which are not burdensome but delightful, are given to explore the other person's innermost thoughts and ways.

I've enjoyed this in my marriage with Lisa. When we were first wed, I didn't know a lot of her longings, delights, favorites, dislikes, or even what she despised. It took a searching out over time—which I've thoroughly enjoyed—to come to know these innermost thoughts and ways. Simply put, it takes focused mental, emotional, and physical effort to grow intimate with your spouse.

The next word of interest in the above verse is *know*; it is the Hebrew word *yāḍa*. In the Old Testament, it's most frequently used to convey intimacy. It's used in Genesis 4:1 when we read, "Adam *knew* [*yāḍa*] Eve his wife, and she conceived" (NKJV). The Holy Spirit uses *yāḍa* to identify the closest that two human beings can become in this life. In essence, David is saying, "Lord, you know me very deeply."

David uses both words, *ḥāqar* and *yāḍa*, to give us the vivid imagery of God searching and seeking out the innermost desires and ways of those He longs to be close with. Again, in looking at Lisa's and my relationship, I know so much more about her after years of spending time together. I not only know her inner desires as mentioned above, but also her routines, how she'll react under certain circumstances, what she enjoys for leisure time, what she loves working on, and the list continues. In the same way, David expounds:

> You know when I sit down or stand up. You know my thoughts even when I'm far away. You see me when I travel and when I rest at home. You know everything I do. You know what I am going to say even before I say it, LORD. (Psalm 139:2–4)

God knows our intimate details beyond comprehension. By *ḥāqar* God exerted Himself to explore, search, and seek out David, and He does the same with each of us—similar, but at such a greater level to what I've done the past forty years with Lisa. In fact, just a few verses later we come to the startling statement that God's thoughts toward us as individuals outnumber every grain of sand (v. 18). If I had pondered Lisa's likes, mannerisms, long-ings, and dislikes every twelve seconds for the past forty years and attached one grain of sand to each thought, it would constitute less than a shoebox full of sand! God's thoughts toward each one of us outnumber every grain of sand *on the planet*, and He would never exaggerate, for that would be a lie, and it is impossible for God to lie. This is mind-blowing! Are you beginning to grasp His passion to know everything about us?

He deeply desires to be close with each of us. Yet allow me to reiter-ate that true intimacy is spawned from *both* parties knowing each other well, not just one. Just as He searches our innermost thoughts, even so we should passionately seek to create true intimacy. Moses pursues this level of relationship by crying out,

> "You have told me, 'I *know* [*yāḍa*] you by name, and I look favorably on you.' If it is true that you look favorably on me, let me *know* [*yāḍa*] your ways so I may understand you more fully and continue to enjoy your favor." (Exodus 33:12–13)

God doesn't *know* us as merely a number amid a mass of people; He knows us personally, individually, by name. In the above verse we see that Moses wants this reciprocated; his passionate desire is to go further in his knowledge of God. He wants a relationship of intimacy—not only God deeply knowing him but also Moses deeply knowing God. So what about us? We are told: "Come close to God, and God will come close to you" (James 4:8).

With what we've just discussed, I think you now hear a call—no, a cry—coming from the heart of God. With each passing moment it intensifies. "Why do you remain distant when you could be intimate with Me?" In essence, we are being informed that *we are the ones who determine the level of our intimacy with God*. Let me say it in simpler terms: you determine how close you are with God, not God! So how does the fear of the Lord play into this? We are told:

> The fear of the LORD is the beginning of knowledge. (Proverbs 1:7 NKJV)

The knowledge of what? Is the writer referring to medical, scientific, historical, or another scholarly knowledge? Many of our universities are filled with this knowledge, yet they have little or no fear of God. Does it refer to social or political knowledge? No, the world's ways are foolish to God. Is it knowledge of the Bible? Not at all, for the Pharisees were experts in Scripture but did not fear God and were very displeasing to Him. Our answer is found in these words:

> Fear the LORD, and you will gain knowledge of God. (Proverbs 2:5)

The word *knowledge* is defined by the *Dictionary of Biblical Languages* as "information of a person, with a strong implication of relationship to that person." *Vine's Complete Expository Dictionary* tells us this word implies "to have an intimate experiential knowledge of Him [God]." To simply state what's promised: *the fear of the Lord is the beginning of knowing God intimately.*

The truth is, we haven't even begun to know God on an intimate level unless we fear Him—it's the starting point. If you initiate anything outside of the starting point, you can't complete it. If I begin a 100-meter dash 50 meters ahead of the starting blocks, I'm unable to participate or complete the race. It's no different in our relationship with God—without holy fear, it's impossible to know Him intimately. Thankfully, He has given us a path to know Him intimately, but will we take it?

Remember that by the fear of the Lord we depart from evil or *lawlessness*. With this knowledge, consider that Jesus foretells of a large group of people who will be shocked on the day of judgment. These men and women call Him their Lord but are going to hear Jesus say, "I never *knew* you; depart from Me, you who practice *lawlessness*" (Matthew 7:23 NKJV). The word for *knew* is *ginōskō*; it is the Greek word for *yāḍa*. Jesus will say to those who lack holy fear, "I never intimately knew you." This presents a huge issue that we'll cover in the next chapter.

Making It Personal

Passage: My heart has heard you say, "Come and talk with me." And my heart responds, "LORD, I am coming." (Psalm 27:8)

Point: True intimacy is spawned from both parties knowing each other well, not just one.

Ponder: Think of your favorite person to be with. How well do you know what they are thinking or feeling without an uttered word? How well do you anticipate their response to various situations? Did you just stumble onto this, or did it take time to search out or ponder your close friend's ways? Now consider God's thoughts of you being innumerable. What does this tell you? What would happen if you searched out and pondered God's heart and ways more than your closest friend's?

Prayer: Dear Lord, I realize I've neglected the greatest invitation I've ever received—to be intimate with You. I've allowed so many things to get in the way of taking the time to develop this closeness. With joy, I choose to make a change. When I open my Bible to read, pray, and ponder, may I come to know You on a deep, intimate level. I ask this in Jesus' name, amen.

Profession: I choose to pursue knowing Jesus as deeply as He has chosen to know me.

*There is a path before each
person that seems right,
but it ends in death.*

—PROVERBS 16:25

30 | A DIFFERENT JESUS

Often, in order to better understand a matter, it helps to look at the antithesis of what we seek to know. So before embarking on further discussions of intimacy with God, let's first address its counterpart, illustrated by the following story.

I had just arrived in Hawaii to speak at a leadership conference. My hotel room wasn't ready, so I found a spot to relax under a poolside umbrella. It just so happened a businesswoman attending a different conference was also waiting for her room. We began talking, and once she discovered I was a Christian author and minister, she began to elaborate on her relationship with Jesus.

It didn't take more than a couple of minutes to realize that she didn't know Him. She kept confidently stating what she *believed*, but very little corresponded to what Scripture reveals. I silently asked the Holy Spirit for wisdom, and within moments He revealed what to say.

Once she finished, I asked, "Do you see the man sitting across the pool?"

With a surprised look on her face (most likely from my abruptly changing the subject), she responded, "Why, yes."

I cheerfully said, "His name is Jim, and he's from Fresno, California. He lives on a strict vegan diet. His dream is to be on the United States Olympic water polo team. He works out in both the pool and the gym three hours a day. His hobbies are pickleball, skydiving, and painting. Jim's married to that woman just over there by the hot tub; her name is Beth, and she's ten years younger."

Now intrigued by how well I knew him, she asked, "Is he attending the conference with you?"

I quickly responded, "No ma'am."

She became more curious. "Well, how do you know Jim so well?"

I then turned, looked her in the eyes, and stated, "I've never met him."

Her countenance changed and now showed caution, maybe even concern. Perhaps she wondered if I was a stalker, private detective, or even a government agent?

I let it sit for a moment, then confidently stated, "That's what I *believe* about him."

She was speechless.

I continued, "You just spoke with great confidence of your *belief* of who Jesus is, but almost everything you just said about Him is not true; it's contrary to what the Bible teaches. I know this because I know Him." Our conversation was over by her choice, but she was noticeably shaken.

The apostle Paul makes a startling statement to a church he loves deeply: "You happily put up with whatever anyone tells you, even if they preach a different Jesus" (2 Corinthians 11:4). He doesn't identify a different god, rather, a different Jesus. It's obvious they *believe in* Jesus yet don't actually *know* Him. Why? They believe whatever appeals to their liking and consequently live estranged from the real Jesus. It isn't hard to do; the Lord is invisible, so you can alter His nature to suit your fancy.

The children of Israel do something similar. Coming out of Egypt is a type of being saved from the world. We read, "All of them . . . drank from the spiritual rock that traveled with them, and that rock was Christ. Yet God was not pleased with most of them" (1 Corinthians 10:4–5). There are numerous reasons God is not pleased, but it all boils down to one main point: their disobedience to God's Word—their *lack of holy fear.*

When Moses is on the mountain for forty days, a golden calf is built by Israel's on-site leader, Aaron. We look at this and cry out "Idolatry!" That's correct; however, what many don't realize is Aaron and all the people refer to the calf as *elōhiym.* This word is found 2,606 times in the Old Testament. It can refer to false gods, but nine out of ten times it refers to *Jehovah*—the one true God. For example, it is found thirty-two times in the first chapter of Genesis. The first verse of the Bible reads, "In the beginning *elōhiym* created the heavens and earth."

We can easily confirm whether they are referring to the calf as *elōhiym*—Almighty God—or as *elōhiym*—false god. The proof is found by Aaron's reference to the calf as *Yahweh* (Exodus 32:5). This is the sacred name of our one true God, and it's never used anywhere in the Bible as a false god's name except here. Aaron and the people don't refer to the calf as *osiris*, *baal*, *isis*, or any other false god's name. They proclaim, "This is *Yahweh*, the one who delivered us out of Egypt" (Exodus 32:4, author's paraphrase).

How could they be so errant? Why don't they know the true living God, as Moses does? They saw His miracles; they followed His cloud and pillar of fire. The answer is not complex. Months earlier, when God originally came down on the mountain to introduce Himself, they retreated and cried out to Moses, "Go yourself and listen to what the LORD our God says. Then come and tell us everything he tells you, and we will listen and obey" (Deuteronomy 5:27).

I can only imagine the utter disappointment of Moses. He can't fathom their lack of desire to be in God's presence. How could this be possible? Moses brings this concern to the Lord expecting to find answers, but it's almost certain God's response surprises Moses: "I have heard what the people said to you, and they are right" (Deuteronomy 5:28).

Moses is stunned. He most likely thinks, *Hold on! They're right? For once these guys are actually right!* I imagine his response to God is something like,

"Why can't they come into Your presence and intimately know you as I do?" God answers, but it's heartbreaking:

> "Oh, that they had such a heart in them that *they would fear Me.*" (Deuteronomy 5:29 NKJV)

God laments, if they only walked in holy fear, they would be able to come into His presence and experience a relationship of intimacy. This in turn would empower them to obey, and thus it would go well for them and their children. Then God gives this directive to Moses:

> Go and say to them, "*Return to your tents.*" But as for you, stand here *by Me*, and I will speak to you. (Deuteronomy 5:30–31 NKJV)

This is both heart-wrenching and exhilarating. First the heartbreak. Israel's darkest hour wasn't when they built the calf, nor when they gave an evil report that kept them from the promised land. No, this was their darkest hour. God brought them out of Egypt (the world) for the purpose of bringing them to Himself so they could know Him as He knew them—intimately. However, they passed it up due to their *lack of holy fear.* Tragic!

On the other hand, it was exciting for Moses, for he was invited to stand near God and hear His words directly from His mouth. He was invited into an intimate relationship with God, while the people went back to their tents.

The lady at the pool proclaimed a *different* Jesus, the Corinthians served a *different* Jesus, and Israel followed a *different* Almighty God. Are we seeing a pattern? It's possible for us to create a deity with the given name of Jesus and yet not know the *actual* Jesus at the right hand of God. And what makes it more disconcerting is Israel and the Corinthian church experienced the Lord's manifest power and miracles in their prayers being answered.

So now let's return to the large group of people who will declare Jesus as their Lord at the judgment but tragically hear Him say the same words as Moses heard God say regarding Israel, "Get away from Me." It would behoove us to more closely examine Jesus' prophetic words of what will actually happen to these multitudes. As stated at the beginning of this chapter, it will give us a better understanding of the importance of holy fear in regard to intimacy with our Lord and Master. We will do this in the next chapter.

═══════ Making It Personal ═══════

Passage: It is this Good News that saves you if you continue to believe the message I told you—unless, of course, you believed something that was never true in the first place. (1 Corinthians 15:2)

Point: It's possible to believe with all your heart in someone or something that isn't true.

Ponder: How do I know for sure that I believe in the actual Jesus, instead of a knockoff? Can I know because my leaders teach about Him? But consider, didn't Aaron teach and lead Israel? Can I know for sure because I read the Bible? But consider, didn't the Pharisees do the same? How can I know?

Prayer: Father, in the name of Jesus, I ask to not only know truth but to love the truth. I choose to embrace Your living Word as final authority and to obey it whether I understand it or not. In doing so I have Your promise that I will not be deceived. As I read and obey Your Word, may it read me; may it reveal to me who I am and who my Lord Jesus is. I ask this in Jesus' name, amen.

Profession: I choose to believe the Word of God whether I understand it or not.

*All day long I opened
my arms to a rebellious
people. But they follow
their own evil paths.*

—ISAIAH 65:2

31 | I DON'T KNOW YOU

We will both grasp and appreciate *intimacy with God* more if we continue to look at its counterpart. Our topic in the last chapter, as well as this one, is a tough pill to swallow. However, the scriptural warnings of our discussion are actually gifts of love and protection from our deeply caring Father. The words spoken from Jesus will instill a holy fear that will keep us close to the Giver of life to the end.

Scripture clearly warns in the latter days a gospel would be proclaimed and widely accepted that would offer a counterfeit salvation void of lordship. Simply put, a relationship with Jesus is offered without committing to unconditionally obey His Word. It's the antithesis of holy fear and produces a *fictional Jesus*, no different from the one Paul accused many of the Corinthians of embracing.

After Paul confronts these Greek "believers" for following a *different Jesus*, he then addresses the state of their hearts that produced the imaginary savior. He writes, "Many of you have not given up your old sins. You have not repented of your impurity, sexual immorality, and eagerness for lustful pleasure" (2 Corinthians 12:21). They profess the Lord Jesus but live contrary to His Word.

This was a rare occurrence in the early church but is widespread in our modern Western church. The consequence of this teaching reduces "Lord" to merely a title rather than a position He holds in people's lives. Jesus prophesies:

> "Not everyone who says to Me, 'Lord, Lord,' shall enter the kingdom of heaven, but he who does the will of My Father in heaven." (Matthew 7:21 NKJV)

Jesus acknowledges people who declare Him as their Lord—not those who revere Mohammad, Joseph Smith, Buddha, Hare Krishna, Confucius, or any other false prophet of our era. Notice *Lord* is consecutively repeated in this verse. Again, if a word or phrase is repeated twice in Scripture, it is not accidental. The writer is communicating emphasis. However, in cases such as this, it's not just emphasis but intensity of emotion. For example, when news reached King David of his son's execution by Joab's army, his response was emotionally charged: "But the king covered his face, and the king *cried out with a loud voice*, 'O my son Absalom! O Absalom, my son, my son!'" (2 Samuel 19:4). He didn't necessarily say "my son" twice; rather, his emotional outcry of grief was so intense that the writer repeated his words.

In the same way the Master is communicating these people's strong sentiments for Him. They are not merely in agreement with the teaching of Jesus Christ being the Son of God; they are emotionally invested and passionate in their belief. We are talking of people who are excited to be "Christians," most likely those who show emotions when speaking of their faith and even weep during a worship service.

Not only do they feel deeply for the cause of Christ, but they also are involved in His service:

> I can see it now—at the Final Judgment thousands strutting up to me and saying, "Master, we preached the Message, we bashed the demons, our super-spiritual projects had everyone talking." (Matthew 7:22 MSG)

I use *The Message* paraphrase because it conveys best that they are not sideliners. They are directly involved in or support the work of their churches. They also are outspoken in their belief of the gospel—"We preached the Message." In essence, they were a part of changing people's lives for the better.

This paraphrased version uses the word *thousands*, but most every other translation uses the word *many*. It's the Greek word *polus*, defined as "much of number, quantity, amount," and often the word is used in the sense of "mostly." In any case, Jesus is not referring to a small group of people but to a vast group who believe in the teachings of the Gospels. They call Him Lord, are emotionally invested, give voice to His message, and are active in Christian service. We would easily identify them as true Christians. So what's the separating factor? How do they differ from authentic believers? Jesus tells us:

> "And then I will declare to them, 'I never *knew* you; depart from Me, you who *practice* lawlessness!'" (Matthew 7:23 NKJV)

The key statement is "*practice* lawlessness." Again, lawless behavior does not adhere to the authority of God's Word. These men and women don't *periodically* stumble; rather, when it serves them better, they habitually ignore, neglect, or disobey God's Word—they lack holy fear.

It's interesting to note that Jesus declared, "I never *knew* you." As stated in a previous chapter, the word *knew* is the Greek word *ginōskō*, which is the same as the Hebrew word *yāḏa*: to intimately know someone. They've never had a true relationship of intimacy with Him. Even though they call Him Master and Lord, it's only a title because they didn't obey His commands. John writes:

> We can be sure that we know [*ginōskō*] him if we obey his command-ments. If someone claims, "I know [*ginōskō*] God," but doesn't obey God's commandments, that person is a liar and is not living in the truth. (1 John 2:3–4)

This perfectly aligns with how Jesus set up His discourse: "You can identify people by their actions" (Matthew 7:20). The actions are not Christian service, speaking the message, or attending church, for those who are turned away will have these qualities.

Let me say it like this: you will certainly find these qualities in a true believer; in fact, a person cannot be a true believer without them. However, possessing these qualities doesn't mean they are a genuine child of God. The deciding factor: are they obedient to His words?

This discussion is Jesus' closing subject in His famous Sermon on the Mount. To put a cap on His startling words, He concludes with:

> "Therefore whoever hears these sayings of Mine, *and does them*, I will liken him to a wise man who built his house on the rock: and the rain descended, the floods came, and the winds blew and beat on that house; and it did not fall, for it was founded on the rock.
>
> But everyone who hears these sayings of Mine, and *does not do them*, will be like a foolish man who built his house on the sand: and the rain descended, the floods came, and the winds blew and beat on that house; and it fell. And great was its fall." (Matthew 7:24–27 NKJV)

If you examine the two groups, it all comes down to one simple difference. He states that both groups hear His words, but the first group *does them*; the second group *does not do them*—or we could say, the first group *trembles at God's Word* (fears God) and the second group *does not tremble at God's Word* (does not fear God).

Jesus makes it clear that these two groups are very similar in appearance. In the group lacking foundation, their belief in the doctrine of Christianity, fervently calling Him their Lord, and their active Christian service represent how they built their life, their house. The solid-foundation group had all the same qualities, except they obeyed His words as if they were their own will. Both houses are made of the same material, the same teachings. They both look identical in worship and service. The difference

I Don't Know You

is the foundation—the unseen. One group privately experiences intimacy with God; the other group doesn't.

Intimacy with God is promised to those who walk in holy fear. In the next several chapters we will see this magnificent privilege you and I are invited into.

Making It Personal

Passage: May God give you more and more *grace* . . . By his divine power [*grace*], God has given us everything we need for living a godly life . . . he has given us great and precious promises. These are the promises that enable you to share his divine nature and escape the world's corruption caused by human desires. (2 Peter 1:2–4)

Point: The evidence that someone is in relationship with Jesus is that they are empowered beyond their own ability to keep His Word. This empowerment is identified as His grace.

Ponder: Am I trying to obey the words of Jesus in my own strength or am I relying on His grace, promises, and divine nature to do so? How can I rely more on His ability, rather than my own?

Prayer: Father, forgive me for attempting to obey Your Word in my own strength. From this moment forward I declare Jesus as the supreme Lord of my life. Whatever Your Word says is final authority in my life. I will depend solely on Your empowering grace and imparted divine nature to walk in Your ways. This is a path we will travel together in close relationship. I'm so grateful for Your invitation to this magnificent life. In Jesus' name, amen.

Profession: I will walk by faith in His ability. No longer will I depend on my ability but will now cooperate with His empowerment.

We're never enlightened or surprised by what comes from our own thoughts. But when God speaks, there's always an element of wonderment and awe.

—JOY DAWSON

32 | THE SECRET OF THE LORD

The past two chapters have been difficult, challenging, and sobering. It's both gut-wrenching and heartbreaking to know that many who expect to hear Jesus say, "Enter into the joy of the Lord," will instead hear, "Depart from Me." There's no greater deception than to think you are in relationship with God when, in fact, you're not. These men and women will suddenly come to the terrible revelation of their foolishness in "using God," instead of being "united with Him." They used His Word for their self-serving purposes instead of experiencing the magnificent love revealed in obeying His Word. With great love Jesus forewarns of this horrible occurrence in order to protect us from slipping into a lukewarm or deceived state.

Now with an understanding of the counterpart of intimacy, let's joyfully begin our discussion of the beauty of being genuinely close with our Creator. We'll begin by looking at a scenario that will take the next few chapters to fully investigate.

To set it up, let me pose a question: Is it possible to be a member of the kingdom (to not hear the horrifying words "depart from Me") but still have missed the opportunity to be intimate with God? The quick answer is yes. But let's explore this in Scripture, and to begin, I'll share one of my favorites:

The *secret* of the Lord is with those who fear Him, and He will show them His covenant. (Psalm 25:14 NKJV)

The Hebrew word for *secret* is *sôḏ* and is defined as "counsel." The Greek dictionary also states, "Confidentiality is at the heart of this term." So in essence, the psalmist isn't talking about one secret but rather God's *secret counsel*, or for our purposes, we will simply call it *secrets* (plural). The scripture could read, "God shares His secrets with those who fear Him."

Now ask yourself this question: Who do you share your secrets with, acquaintances or close friends? I'm certain you answered close friends. God is no different; He shares His secrets with intimate, close friends, and His close friends are those who embrace holy fear. The ESV reads: "The friendship of the Lord is for those who fear him."

God is not everyone's friend. Let me restate it more specifically: *God is not a friend to everyone who is in the church.* To expand on this, let's begin in the Old Testament. There are two men identified as God's friend: Abraham and Moses. Are there others? Absolutely—Noah, Daniel, Esther, Joseph, David, Job, Enoch, Isaiah, and many more walked closely with God. However, these two men's lives exemplify the path that leads to a relationship of friendship with the Lord.

Let's begin with Abraham. Why is he called God's friend? When he was seventy-five years old, God promised to grant his heart's greatest desire, a son. However, it wasn't immediate. He waited twenty-five more years before Sarah, his wife, miraculously gave birth to Isaac. Can you imagine the profound appreciation and immense sweetness in waiting that long for this fulfillment?

I'm certain the father-son relationship grew stronger with each passing year. His great wealth was nothing compared to his delight in his son. Nothing meant more to Abraham—not even his own life.

But then one day, with no advanced warning whatsoever, God says to Abraham in prayer, "Take your son, your only son—yes, Isaac, whom you love so much—and go to the land of Moriah. Go and sacrifice him as a burnt offering on one of the mountains, which I will show you" (Genesis 22:2).

What?! Kill the most important person or thing in your life, just because God said to do it and didn't give you a reason? Are you serious! Can you imagine Abraham's shock at hearing these words? Never could he have imagined that God would ask such a difficult thing of him. He'd requested more than even Abraham's life—He had asked for his heart. It made no sense.

Let me interject this important point: *we* know it was a test. In fact, Scripture makes it clear, "Some time later, God tested Abraham's faith" (v. 1). But herein lies the disadvantage of reading a historical account that has already played out—we know the outcome; most believers have heard it or read it several times. But we forget that Abraham did not know it was a test! We never know when God is testing us until we are on the other side of it. It may be possible to cheat on a high school test, but no one can cheat on the exams God gives. If we haven't done our homework of abiding in His Word for the purpose of sanctifying our hearts, we'll be hard-pressed to pass, no matter how clever we are!

If Abraham's descendants had known the occasions of God's tests in the wilderness, they would have responded differently. Abraham had something different, something his descendants lacked: holy fear.

I love Abraham's response to God's extremely difficult command: "The next morning Abraham got up early" (Genesis 22:3). He got right to it! He didn't mull it over for a few days or weeks; he didn't call on his friends to get their opinion. He didn't ignore or resist God's command. He, Isaac, and two servants got up early the next morning, packed up, and started on their way.

It may have been slightly easier to act after hearing God's voice the night before, but what about two and a half days later, when Abraham hasn't heard a word from heaven since, and he is now face-to-face with the mountain on which he will sacrifice his most important person or possession, just because God said to do it, with no reason provided?

Abraham continues to the foot of the mountain and asks his servants to wait. He takes Isaac up the mountain and builds the altar, all the while hiding his turbulent emotions and tears. It has taken every bit of his willpower and mental strength to carry out what was needed for the sacrifice. The critical moment arrives; all hope seems lost for God to change His mind. So in great anguish he ties up Isaac, lifts the knife, and is ready to thrust it into his son's heart—all because God asked. No reason was given.

Suddenly, an angel of God appears and cries out, "Do not lay your hand on the lad, or do anything to him; for *now I know that you fear God*, since you have not withheld your son, your only son, from Me" (Genesis 22:12 NKJV).

How did the angel know that Abraham feared God? Because he obeyed *instantly*, when it *didn't make sense*, when he *didn't see a benefit*, when it *hurt*, and he did it to *completion*.

Abraham then puts down the knife, unties Isaac, lifts his eyes, and sees a ram caught in a bush. Out of his mouth come these words: "Jehovah-Jireh," which means, "the Lord will provide" (Genesis 22:14). What just happened? In that moment, God revealed a facet of His character to Abraham that no one else had known before. Why? Because he's God's friend.

Let me clarify. All of you reading this book know me as John Bevere, the author. Some of you who have heard me speak in conferences or churches know me as John Bevere, the public speaker. However, there is a woman—her name is Lisa—who knows me as John Bevere, husband; John Bevere, dad; John Bevere, granddad; John Bevere, best friend; John Bevere, lover; and I could continue. Very few people know these facets of my personality—only those closest to me. And the final one, only Lisa knows.

Abraham became a closer friend to God that day, and in the next chapter we will explore the extraordinary dynamics between these two friends—and how we, too, can have a relationship like that.

Making It Personal

Passage: The secret [of the sweet, satisfying companionship] of the Lord have they who fear (revere and worship) Him, and He will show them His covenant *and* reveal to them its [deep, inner] meaning. (Psalm 25:14 AMPC)

Point: God shares His secrets with close friends, and His close friends are those who embrace holy fear.

Ponder: What is a friend? How do friends enjoy life together? What makes a friendship deeper? Would I like to be a friend of God? What do I think He is looking for in a friend? Have I been a good friend to Him? If not, what should change? What are my desires in being His friend?

Prayer: Dear Lord, I desire to be one of Your intimate friends. I know this is also Your desire. In pondering what a close friend is, I realize I've not been a faithful friend to You. Please forgive me for not placing Your desires above all else and protecting our relationship in the way I live and respond to You. I ask for the grace to be Your friend for all eternity. In Jesus' name, amen.

Profession: I will seek to be a friend to God and choose to make nothing else a greater priority.

The fear of God illumines the soul, annihilates evil, weakens the passions, drives darkness from the soul and makes it pure. The fear of God is the summit of wisdom. Where it is not you will find nothing good. Whoever does not have the fear of God is open to diabolical falls.

—EPHREM THE SYRIAN

33 | THE INSIDE SCOOP

We've discussed how the friendship between God and Abraham formed. It's an example of how we can enter a similar relationship of intimacy with God. But, before we address that, let's continue with Abraham. We read:

> Don't you remember that our ancestor Abraham was shown to be right with God *by his actions* when he offered his son Isaac on the altar? . . . He was even *called the friend of God*. (James 2:21, 23)

The apostle James speaks of their friendship, and it's no coincidence that both James's and the angel's words agree. What fostered this closeness was Abraham's holy fear, and it was made evident by his quick and complete obedience (actions). Even when the command didn't make sense, had no apparent benefit attached, and was painful to carry out, he trembled at God's Word. Godly fear motivates us both to *will* and to *do* what God asks of us. It opens the door to intimacy with Him.

On a certain day God directed this question to the two angels that accompanied Him on a visit with Abraham near the oak grove belonging to Mamre: "Should I hide My plan from Abraham?" (Genesis 18:17).

The Lord then turned to Abraham to discuss His intentions, and the two angels went on to the cities of Sodom and Gomorrah. I'm going to paraphrase what happens next for relatability, but in essence the Lord said, "Abraham, I'm planning to blow up these two cities because the outcry of their sin is so flagrant. What do you think?"

Can you imagine hearing these words from the Creator? In shock Abraham replies, "Sodom?!"

The Lord responds, "Yes, yes, and Gomorrah too. What are your thoughts on this matter?"

In a panic Abraham says to himself: *Think, Abraham, think. My nephew Lot is down there, so I have to intercede on his behalf as well as any other innocent people.* Abraham comes up with an idea:

> Will you sweep away both the righteous and the wicked? Suppose you find fifty righteous people living there in the city—will you still sweep it away and not spare it for their sakes? Surely you wouldn't do such a thing, destroying the righteous along with the wicked. Why, you would be treating the righteous and the wicked exactly the same! Surely you wouldn't do that! Should not the Judge of all the earth do what is right? (Genesis 18:23–25)

Can you imagine God's joy and pleasure to hear His covenant man's response? He most likely responded, "Excellent point! Okay, I'll not destroy the two cities if there are fifty righteous people there. I'm so glad I talked to My friend Abraham."

But Abraham isn't satisfied—what if there aren't fifty? So he repeats the matter but reduces the number to forty-five.

The Lord replies, "Another good point! Okay, I'll not destroy the cities if there are forty-five righteous people. Glad I had this discussion with My friend Abraham."

Abraham doesn't stop; he keeps pressing the matter, moving from forty-five to forty, then to thirty, then to twenty, and finally to ten righteous people. He thinks to himself, *There has to be ten. Lot, my nephew, is one—all that's needed is nine others.*

Only a friend can talk this way to a king who has the power to execute judgment. Coming from a servant or subject, such a petition would be disrespectful. The Lord agreed to each request, and then we read: "When the LORD had finished His conversation with Abraham, He went on His way, and Abraham returned to his tent" (Genesis 18:33).

Remember, fearing God means that we love what He loves and hate what He hates. God once spoke to me on a certain day after I reached out in love to speak healing words to someone who had been harsh with me: "Son, when you care about what I care about—people—then I will discuss My plans with you." Holy fear actually enables us to love more truly and more deeply not only God but also people.

Scripture states that those in Sodom and Gomorrah were "eating and drinking, buying and selling, farming and building" (Luke 17:28). Let's put it in more relatable vernacular: "Life is good, the economy is booming, and if there is a God, He doesn't mind our lifestyle." These cities were less than twenty-four hours away from being obliterated, and the people were clueless. But this is not the most alarming reality.

The terrifying reality is this: Lot, whom the Bible identifies as "a righteous man" (2 Peter 2:7), was equally clueless about what was about to happen—no different than all the ungodly people! It took two angels of mercy to get him and his family out—all because Abraham prayed (Genesis 19:29).

To make this story more relevant, let's look at it as if it happened in our time. We have two *righteous* men—two saved, born-again Christian men. One *righteous* man knows what God is going to do before He does it, and helps God decide how He's going to do it. The other righteous man is as clueless to the impending judgment as the wicked. Why? The first righteous man fears God; therefore, he's a friend of God who, in turn, knows the secrets of God. The second righteous man does not fear God; therefore, he's not a friend of God, and so he does not know the secrets of God.

Lot was called righteous, but he was worldly. He represents the believer who, when forced into the corner, seeks first to serve his or her own best interests, similar to the Corinthian church, similar to many in our Western church. This group of "righteous" men and women have a relationship with God that is not too different from my relationship with the president of the United States. I may benefit from his decisions and leadership, but I don't know the inside scoop, his plans, his personal feelings, or his decisions before he makes them.

Lot's character is made evident by where he chose to dwell, the type of wife he chose, and the children he fathered through incest—the Moabites and Ammonites. Lot originally chose what looked best to him. When parting ways, Abraham had given him first choice of what land to live in, agreeing to go the opposite direction. Scripture states, "Lot took a *long look* at the fertile plains of the Jordan Valley" (Genesis 13:10). Why the long look? He knew the wickedness of the cities in those plains. He was most likely trying to determine how he could enjoy the benefits of the world's system, but not get caught up in it. He devised a plan. He chose to camp on the plains, a safe distance from the hub of wickedness (Genesis 13:12), but his compromising idea didn't work. Later he and his family ended up inside the gates of the city; he was eventually drawn in.

When we lack holy fear, we'll inevitably seek to get as close to the world as possible without falling headlong into it. However, if this is our motive, it is only a matter of time before the world draws us in. We must remember we are called into the world to reach the lost, not to be part of them.

Lot's life serves as a warning to each of us. The day of judgment would have come upon Lot as a thief in the night had it not been for Abraham's intercession. There were terrible consequences for his worldliness. As stated, Lot's offspring were very ungodly. His wife was so attached to Sodom that she disobeyed the angels' command to not look back, and it resulted in judgment—she instantly became a pillar of salt. In love, Jesus warns us to "remember what happened to Lot's wife!" (Luke 17:32).

Now it is wise to ask, is this condition of friendship true for those of us who are God's children? We'll address it shortly, but first, let's examine the other noted friend of God in the Old Testament.

Making It Personal

Passage: Come close to God, and God will come close to you. Wash your hands, you sinners; purify your hearts, for your loyalty is divided between God and the world. (James 4:8)

Point: God shares His plans with those who fear Him. He hides His plans from those whose loyalty is divided between God and the world.

Ponder: Jesus states, "When He, the Spirit of truth, has come . . . He will tell you things to come" (John 16:13 NKJV). How does this correlate with how God and Abraham interacted? Is this something I desire with God, for Him to share His plans with me?

Prayer: Dear Lord, I desire to hear Your secret counsel. I realize I've flirted with the world as Lot did. I've in essence removed myself from Your inner counsel. I repent of this. I ask You to thoroughly cleanse me with the blood of Jesus my Lord. Please receive me as one You share Your counsel with. In Jesus' name, amen.

Profession: I choose God over the world.

Only when we are captured by an overwhelming sense of awe and reverence in the presence of God, will we begin to worship God in spirit and in truth.

—ALISTAIR BEGG

34 | FACE TO FACE

Let's now look at the other Old Testament man who is referred to as "friend" in his relationship with God.

> So the LORD spoke to Moses *face to face*, as a man speaks to his *friend*. (Exodus 33:11 NKJV)

It's almost incomprehensible that Scripture uses the phrase "face to face" in describing God and Moses' shared friendship. Keep in mind, this is God Almighty, not someone down the street, or even a famous figure. Are you grasping the magnitude of this statement? This term of intimacy isn't used just once; it's used a second time when the Lord was angry with Aaron and Miriam for criticizing Moses. He sternly declares:

> "Of all my house, he is the one I *trust*. I speak to him *face to face*, clearly, and not in riddles! He sees the LORD as he is." (Numbers 12:7–8)

For God to say "I trust you" is one of the greatest compliments a human being can receive. This offers more insight into having friendship with God—the foundation of trust. What builds trust with God?

Unconditional obedience—always doing what's asked

Absolute integrity—always keeping your word
Unwavering priority—always putting His desires first
Knowing His heart—always choosing God's will when making
　　decisions

Consistency in all four is paramount. If one area is broken, quick and sincere repentance puts you on the path of regained trust. Holy fear motivates this reliability in all four categories, and Moses exuded a high level of it. In this chapter, we'll focus on the third and fourth category—in essence always knowing and choosing God's heart.

Consider Moses' life—his first forty years were filled with great wealth, the finest foods, fashionable clothing, the best material possessions, and any desirable pleasure. He lived in a spectacular home; no one on earth was more wealthy or powerful than his grandfather, the pharaoh. Yet we read:

He *chose* . . . to suffer for the sake of Christ [rather] than to own the treasures of Egypt, for he was looking ahead to *his great reward*. (Hebrews 11:25–26)

Moses *chose* to walk away from it all. He could have attempted to serve God in the palace, but he sought a *reward* that staying in Egypt couldn't provide. Was it the promised land? It couldn't have been, for what did the land of milk and honey have to offer that he didn't already possess?

To discover what he sought most, let's consider his life after the palace. Did his choice to leave it all seem wise? Were his life conditions better than being a prince in Egypt? He left ruling people for tending sheep in the wilderness for forty years! That's a long time—tending sheep! Next, he experienced a very stressful and lengthy process of freeing God's people from Pharaoh. If all that weren't enough, now he finds himself living in a tent in an arid desert filled with great challenges. The people he's leading are disgruntled, combative, and utterly dissatisfied with his leadership.

In the midst of this, God makes an offer to Moses that will alleviate much of the stress and turmoil. He instructs Moses to round up the people and take them to the promised land. He assigns a choice angel to guide them and drive out all the opposing nations. The Lord reminds Moses that it will be a rich, fertile land, but finally declares, "But I will not go with you myself" (Exodus 33:3 GNT).

Pause and consider what Moses and the people faced daily. They've had no variety—no beautiful valleys, rivers, forests, fertile soil, gardens, orchards, or pastures. No one's taken a warm bath, slept in a comfortable bed, worn fresh clothing, or enjoyed a shopping market for quite some time. Their menu is utterly boring: no fresh fruits or vegetables, no fish or beef, no desserts, just bread that appears on the ground each morning with no accompanying peanut butter, jam, or cold cuts—nothing else!

Slavery in Egypt was awful but wandering in the arid desert wasn't any better; both conditions were extremely difficult, though in different ways. However, in the desert, the Israelites have a hope: their own land—a rich, fertile, and beautiful land. They've waited for it for generations!

Can you imagine hearing God's wonderful words? Surely Moses will accept, hurry down the mountain, and announce the grand news to the national assembly. The people will celebrate, laud him as a great leader once again, and everyone will happily begin their long-awaited journey to the much-anticipated promised land. However, listen to Moses' reply to God's offer:

> "If you don't personally go with us, don't make us leave *this place*." (Exodus 33:15)

As a reminder, where was "this place"? It was the place of adversity, stress, and hardship. Moses gave a reply that is perplexing, even mind-boggling, to the unenlightened. In essence he declared, "If I have to choose between Your *presence* and Your *blessings*, I'll take Your presence!" Why? You can know about someone in their absence but not become close and intimate. This was Moses' coveted reward.

You may question, why would God be pleased with Moses refusing what he was told to do? Moses knew God's heart. Consider this: have you ever offered someone you loved the opportunity to go and do something benefi-cial or pleasurable for only them, and sincerely meant it, but they surprised you by saying, "No, my preference is to be with you, rather than enjoy it without you." A response like this is rare, overwhelming, and most wonderful.

Moses feared God, so what was important to God was consistently his priority; he had God's heart, and thus, His trust. The people he led had a different heart. We read:

> He [God] revealed his *character* to Moses and his *deeds* to the people of Israel. (Psalm 103:7)

Just as with Abraham, God revealed his *character* to Moses. The Good News Translation of the Bible states that God revealed His *plans* to Moses. In other words, His private secrets were revealed to Moses, but not to Israel. Israel only knew God by how He answered their prayers—His *deeds*.

How many believers today only know God by answered prayers? Their relationship with Him is more transactional, not intimate. They know His words, but not His heart. Scripture often seems like rules and historical stories, or it's used merely as a source of inspiration. Even worse, it's twisted to grant permission to practice lawless behavior instead of offering life-transforming truths revealing His heart.

Both Moses and Israel were righteous, no different from Abraham and Lot. However, only those who fear God are entitled to know His heart—character, secrets, and plans. Why would God trust Moses but not His people? Because God knew Moses would always choose God's heart over what looked best for him—this is holy fear.

When Israel built the calf in Exodus, God in a rage declared:

> "Now leave me alone so my fierce anger can blaze against them, and I will destroy them. Then I will make you, Moses, into a great nation." (32:10)

Once again, a remarkable offer is made—to make Moses a great nation. Incredible. How did Moses respond? Once again, he chose what was best for God, not himself. He boldly challenged this proposal by reminding God of His reputation with Egypt and the watching world—others would say God wasn't faithful to His people. The interaction became so intense that Moses bluntly stated, "Change your mind!" (v. 12). He had the guts to tell God, when He was furious, to change His mind! This cannot happen unless you fear God and consequently know His heart and desire His best.

This is why God trusted Moses and didn't trust the people, even though He'd saved every one of them. He powerfully delivered the people from Egypt's strong grip, but He wouldn't share His heart with them. Does this condition of friendship apply to God's children in New Testament times? We'll see in the next chapter.

Making It Personal

Passage: All things have been *entrusted* and delivered to Me by My Father . . . and no one fully knows and accurately understands the Father except the Son. (Matthew 11:27 AMPC)

Point: For God to say "I trust you" is one of the greatest compliments a human being can receive. The foundation of trust is imperative to entering a friendship with God; it is found in those who fear the Lord.

Ponder: Moses feared God, knew His heart, and was trusted by God. Jesus delighted in the fear of the Lord, knew His Father's heart, and was entrusted with all things. What is the correlation? What happens when we delight in holy fear?

Prayer: Dear Lord, I desire to be trusted by You. Please forgive me for the times I've not obeyed You, not kept my word, not put Your desires and what's best for You above my desires. I choose to change this and ask that You would fill me with holy fear to empower me to make this life change. I ask this in Jesus' name, amen.

Profession: I choose to be one who can be trusted by my Lord Jesus.

Did not our heart burn within us while He talked with us on the road, and while He opened the Scriptures to us?

—LUKE 24:32 NKJV

35 | YOU ARE MY FRIENDS

The lives of Abraham and Moses exemplify what's necessary to enter a relationship of friendship with God. The Lord went as far as to say of Moses, "*Of all my house*, he is the one I trust" (Numbers 12:7). In that generation, God declared there wasn't anyone else among His people whom He could trust more. What a startling statement.

Did Jesus alter this criterion? Did He open up a relationship of friendship to all who believe in Him? The quick answer is no, but let's investigate by opening with a statement John writes at the onset of Jesus' ministry:

> Because of the miraculous signs Jesus did in Jerusalem at the Passover celebration, many began to *trust* in him. But Jesus didn't *trust* them, because he knew all about people. (John 2:23–24)

The word *trust* is an interesting Greek word that is defined as "to believe to the extent of complete trust and reliance—to have confidence in, to have faith in."[1] Interestingly, this trust is not reciprocated by Jesus. Even though people believed to the extent of complete trust in and reliance on Him, He didn't trust them. He knew a vast many human beings were not reliable. He loved them and served them but did not hold them at the level of friendship. The trust that God attributed to Moses was not extended by Jesus (God manifested in the flesh) to those who simply believed in Him.

Let's move forward to the Last Supper. In the previous three years of ministry, most who believed in Him were not reliable; many followed secretly or from a distance or only when it benefited them. Many disciples left Him, and Judas betrayed Him.[2] Does this give more insight as to why Jesus didn't reciprocate the trust?

At the supper, Jesus is now sitting with those closest to Him. With gratitude and affection, He says, "You are those who have stayed with me in my trials" (Luke 22:28 ESV). In essence, they had been reliable. Peter would have a major hiccup later that evening but would repent and return with an even more loyal heart, and Jesus knew it.

Judas has left to carry out the betrayal, and Jesus says of the eleven remaining, "No longer do I call you servants" (John 15:15 NKJV). The fact that Jesus says "No longer" means that these men were at one time regarded as servants. This is not revelation, just simple English. Paul expounds this principle in writing:

As long as an heir is a minor, he's not really much different than a servant. (Galatians 4:1 TPT)

We must ask, why does God keep us at the level of a servant when we are heirs of His kingdom? The answer: to protect us! He doesn't desire Ananias and Sapphira's plight to be ours; He takes no pleasure in this.

In the 1980s, Lisa and I worked for two global ministries, one with a paid staff of 450 employees and the other with 150. We saw leadership issues we didn't care for in both, and once we started our own ministry, we swung the pendulum to the opposite end of how to lead our staff. Some ideas were good, but others weren't. One paradigm we initiated was, "I am going to be every employee's best friend." You may already recognize the stupidity of this wisdom.

Our first employee was a young man I'll call Justin. I made him my best buddy; we played basketball together, watched videos together, ate together frequently, and all the other activities best friends do. It was great at first. However, after a year I had to offer him some minor correction. He sat across my desk, and I opened the conversation by gently saying, "Justin, when you travel with me, you need to treat the people who come to our resource table kindly. Please smile and interact with them because they are precious to God."

What happened next shocked me. He pointed his finger and started accusing me of all kinds of errant behavior. He listed things I was doing incorrectly. I thought, *Oh no, am I doing these things?* But a few minutes into it, I recognized he was seeing me through critical eyes. I paused and asked the Holy Spirit what to do. He softly spoke, "Release him from the ministry."

I let him fully vent before I said, "Justin, I need to release you from our staff."

He was furious, and he stormed out of our home. I immediately teared up, because I cared for him. Suddenly the Holy Spirit whispered, "He'll be back and will be twice as faithful."

Three months later I got a call from Justin. He said, "God has spoken clearly to me and brought correction. I am calling to ask your forgiveness. I lost sight of where God put me in your and Lisa's life, and I lost sight of the position where He had put you both in my life. I treated you both as common, ordinary—as peers and not as leaders. I'm so sorry."

I quickly responded, "Justin, I forgive you." After more conciliatory comments, I asked if he would return to work for us. He happily agreed, and we never had problems in that area again.

Now I have a different mindset. I refrain from sharing the intimate secrets of my heart with any employee until I know they are established in what Justin lost sight of. I don't do this to be aloof or impersonal with our team members; I do it to protect them. I don't want them to experience what happened to Justin. However, once I know an employee is established in our positions, I then bring them in as a friend. Some of our team members are my closest friends.

In essence, the Lord says to us, "Until you are very established in who I am in your life and very established in who you are with Me—the fear of the Lord—I need to keep you at a servant level even though you are an heir—a son or daughter of My kingdom. This is to protect you, so you don't experience judgment similar to Ananias and Sapphira."

Jesus says to these men:

> No longer do I call you *servants*, for a servant does not know what his master is doing; but I have called you *friends*, for all things that I heard from My Father I have made known to you. (John 15:15 NKJV)

Jesus is essentially saying, "Up to now I have not given you the inside scoop—My plans, secret counsel, or intimate areas of My heart. But now I can *trust* you as I did with Moses and Abraham." This is why Jesus states to all of us:

> "You are My friends *if* . . ." (John 15:14 NKJV)

We sing songs, preach sermons, and speak casually about Jesus being our friend, and some even go so far as to refer to Him as if he were a buddy. However, we rarely finish His statement. The word "if" is a condition; it's not automatic, even if we believe in Him. What is the condition of friendship?

"You are My friends *if you do whatever I command you.*"

There is the condition: *the fear of the Lord*—trembling at His Word, obeying His commands instantly and to completion, even if it doesn't make sense, you don't see the benefit, or it is painful. Just as Abraham and Moses were welcomed into a relationship of friendship with God Almighty due to their awe of God, it is no different with us now. When the Lord's heart and will are our number-one priority, He then can trust us and will welcome us into a relationship of friendship. What an honor, what a privilege, and how exhilarating to be a friend of the Creator of the universe.

Before closing, allow me to address a possible lingering question: Does Jesus give us commands? Yes, there are over five hundred commands in the New Testament alone. These are not commands required for salvation, though, since that's a free gift. Rather, these are commands that glorify God that we are empowered to keep by holy fear. Jesus' final words before leaving were: "Go therefore and make disciples of all the nations . . . teaching them to observe all things that *I have commanded you*" (Matthew 28:19–20 NKJV).

The greatest benefit of holy fear is to be welcomed into a friendship relationship with Jesus. In the next section we'll examine other benefits of holy fear.

================= **Making It Personal** =================

Passage: "You are My friends if you do whatever I command you." (John 15:14 NKJV)

Point: We don't gain Jesus' trust by simply believing in Him. Friendship with the Lord is reserved for those who fear Him.

Ponder: Is it worth it to obey Jesus immediately and completely, even if it doesn't make sense, even if there doesn't seem to be a personal benefit, even if it is painful? Is the benefit of His friendship worth it?

Prayer: Dear Lord, I desire above all else to be one of Your intimate friends. I don't want to know You from afar; I want to be close to You. I choose the fear of the Lord—to obey You unconditionally, to love You with all my heart, soul, body, and strength, and to love people in truth as You do. I ask this in Jesus' name, amen.

Profession: I choose to become a friend of Jesus! I will obey whatever He commands me.

The Treasure's Benefits

WEEK 6

Ponder the path of your feet, and let all your ways be established.

—PROVERBS 4:26 NKJV

36 | ESTABLISHING HIS PROMISES

Now let's turn our attention to the numerous benefits of holy fear. We've discussed several already, including the greatest—intimacy with God. Let's continue to unravel the knowledge of "how great is the goodness [God has] stored up for those who fear [Him]" (Psalm 31:19).

Before we begin this exciting discussion, it's important to clarify a common misunderstanding. Often people interpret Scripture through the lens of experience—either their own or others—rather than allowing Scripture to shape their experience. In essence, God's promises are viewed as "hit or miss" scenarios, with this prevailing thought: *If God wants this for me, that's wonderful. But if not, He is sovereign, and I need to accept it.* This belief sets God up to show partiality with His children, which just isn't true. This can easily create hidden and unspoken resentment against the Lord.

The real story is quite different; often we must contend for what God speaks. To elaborate, we'll turn to Scripture to establish this truth. Let's set up a biblical promise most would consider automatic. God spoke to Abraham, "Isaac is the son through whom your descendants will be counted" (Genesis 21:12). This word from God, along with earlier words, made the divine promise clear: the reality of Abraham being the father of a nation and that the coming Messiah would come through Isaac's offspring.

With this in mind, let's see how Isaac's lineage began, starting with how God picked the girl for him to marry. Abraham's servant travels to his master's homeland to find a bride for Isaac. After a long journey, he stands at the community well and prays for an unmistakable sign from God—the girl who will give water to his ten camels without being asked is "the one *you have selected* as Isaac's wife" (Genesis 24:14).

Let's pause here to note that after a long desert trek one camel can drink anywhere from thirty to fifty gallons of water in fifteen minutes. Multiply that by ten camels, and that's a lot of water for a girl to voluntarily draw. His prayer would have to be answered miraculously, but Rebekah perfectly fulfills his request! There's no doubt, she is divinely selected to be Isaac's wife.

After the servant returns home with Rebekah, Isaac and Rebekah are married. But there is a huge obstacle to the fulfillment of the promise—she's barren and cannot have children! Did God make a mistake? Didn't He know she couldn't conceive? How can the promise be fulfilled? Why would He pick her? What should Isaac and Rebekah do? Should they just wait for the promise to be fulfilled—until her womb one day miraculously opens?

In the search for our answer, let's look to Abraham for our first clue. He is a man of bold prayer. He is the one who challenged God to keep to His nature and not destroy Sodom and Gomorrah for the sake of ten righteous people. We know from Scripture that he teaches his son to do the same (Genesis 18:19). Knowing this we read:

> Isaac *pleaded* with the LORD on behalf of his wife, because she was unable to have children. The LORD *answered Isaac's prayer*, and Rebekah became pregnant with twins. (Genesis 25:21)

Again, if there was a promise of God that was sure to happen without any human involvement, it would have been Rebekah's ability to have babies. But this was not the case. It took a very specific action from Isaac to ensure God's promise. He had to *plead*. The Hebrew dictionary states, "The fundamental meaning of this word is that of a cry to the Lord." So it wasn't just a casual prayer but a fervent petition, one that wouldn't take no for an answer. The kind of prayer that pleases God. We are told:

> The effective, fervent prayer of a righteous man avails much. (James 5:16 NKJV)

The apostle James states that an effective prayer is an earnest or passionate prayer. He gives the example of Elijah praying for rain. Seven times Elijah had to passionately pray, with his head between his knees, and seven times send his servant to the lookout to see if the rain clouds were coming. His faith refused to give up until the promise of God was fulfilled in the earth (1 Kings 18:41–45).

Isaac knew God's will and passionately cried out for it to be established on earth. Is the same true for all believers? We are told:

> Forever, O LORD, Your word is *settled* in heaven. (Psalm 119:89 NKJV)

God's Word is established in heaven. It's not by accident that earth is not mentioned, only heaven. Why? The psalmist states, "The heavens belong to the LORD, but he has given the earth to all humanity" (Psalm 115:16). The Lord owns heaven and earth (1 Corinthians 10:26), but He has leased the earth to mankind for a period of time.

Early in our marriage, Lisa and I leased an apartment. We didn't own it, but it was ours to live in and make our home. The owners didn't come on the premises to override how we set up the furniture, decorated it, or any other aspect of living in it. However, if we called for help, we would get the owner's assistance.

It's a similar arrangement with how God owns earth but has leased it to mankind. This explains why He didn't come into the garden and slap the fruit out of Adam's hand. He gave mankind dominion over the earth (Genesis 1:26–28). With this understanding, we must ask, how does His Word become established on the earth? We are told: "By the *mouth* of two or

three witnesses every word shall be established" (2 Corinthians 13:1 NKJV).
And in Isaiah, God declares:

> So shall My word be that goes forth from My *mouth*; it shall not return to
> Me void, but it shall accomplish what I please. (Isaiah 55:11 NKJV)

Interestingly, in both scriptures the word *mouth* is specified. God's
mouth speaks His desired will, but it takes a human being—who has been
given authority on earth—to speak it out of their mouth to establish it on
earth. In essence we make a request for Him to come and assist on the earth.
Now His promise is established on earth as it is in heaven. Simply put, He
will not force His way into our "leased earth" unless we ask for His will to
be done.

God spoke the promise to Abraham. Can you visualize Isaac pleading,
"God of my father, You promised that a nation would come from me and
my descendants would be blessed. I ask You to open my wife's womb to bear
children. Amen." The result: God's will was established.

Now let's look at our greatest example, Jesus.

> While Jesus was here on earth, he offered prayers and pleadings, with a
> loud cry and tears, to the one who could rescue him from death. And God
> *heard* his prayers because of his deep reverence for God. (Hebrews 5:7)

Again, we encounter the word *pleadings*, but this time it is coupled
with the words *deep reverence for God*. Another key is given. It not only
takes relentless faith, which speaks (cries out)—until the promise of God
is evident on earth—but also the fear of the Lord to establish the promises
made by God to His people. Notice God "heard'" Jesus' prayers. It's one
thing to pray, but it is another matter to be *heard*. Are there prayers that
are not heard? Absolutely. James writes, "When you ask, you don't get it
because your motives are all wrong" (James 4:3). Again, we have to look at
our motives, and the fear of the Lord is what keeps our motives in check.

When we fear God, we can boldly pray and declare God's promises or will to be done on this earth, and it will be established, as in heaven. Could this be why the apostle Paul writes near the end of his time on earth, "Fight the good fight of faith, lay hold on eternal life" (1 Timothy 6:12 NKJV). It's a fight, and by faith we lay hold of what eternal life provides.

Making It Personal

Passage: He grants the desires of those who fear him; he hears their cries. (Psalm 145:19)

Point: Often people interpret Scripture through the lens of experience—either their own or others'—rather than allowing Scripture to shape their experience.

Ponder: Have I allowed my beliefs to drift from what is declared in Scripture due to my own or others' experiences? Are there promises that have not yet been fulfilled in my life, in my family, in my world of influence? Have I settled for living outside of these divine promises? Am I willing to contend for the promises by pleading for them to be fulfilled in this earth?

Prayer: Dear Lord, in Jesus' name, forgive me for spiritual laziness, settling for unfulfilled promises, and not fighting for what Your Word declares. I've looked to past experiences to shape my path rather than contended for Your will to be established. I repent and choose to fight the good fight of faith, to pray for Your will to be established in this earth as it is in heaven. Amen.

Profession: I choose to fight the good fight of faith, to lay hold of what eternal life declares, to see God's will established in my world of influence.

Men who fear God face life fearlessly. Men who do not fear God end up fearing everything.

—RICHARD HALVERSON

37 | THE FEAR THAT ELIMINATES FEARS

We live in a troubled and fear-filled world. In fact, Jesus tells us it will only intensify. His description of what's on the horizon is sobering: "'Men's hearts failing them from fear and the expectation of those things which are coming on the earth'" (Luke 21:26 NKJV). These fears and anxieties displace hope, peace, and tranquility, leaving only unrest, heavy hearts, and persistent torment. What's the antidote?

> The Lord has given me a strong warning not to think like everyone else does. He said, "Don't call everything a conspiracy, like they do, and don't live in dread of what frightens them. Make the Lord of Heaven's Armies holy in your life. He is the one you should fear. He is the one who should make you tremble. He will keep you safe. (Isaiah 8:11–14)

Holy fear eliminates all other fears and anxieties, for it is backed by God's promise of being kept safe. Stop for a moment and ponder this reality.

Imagine all the armed forces of the United States being assigned to protect you. Every general informs their down-line officers that you're top priority, and anything required for your safety is to be implemented. Their full spectrum of advanced weaponry is committed to provide protection wherever you stay or go. It's almost unimaginable, but if this occurred, I'm sure you'd feel safe and secure. Yet this pales in comparison to God Almighty saying, "I will keep you safe." No wonder we are told:

> How great is the goodness you have stored up for those who *fear you*. You lavish it on those who come to you for protection, blessing them before the watching world. You hide them in the shelter of your presence, safe from those who conspire against them. You shelter them in your presence, far from accusing tongues. (Psalm 31:19–20)

The promise of lavished goodness—being hidden in the shelter of God's presence, safe from those who would try to harm us—is not made to all, but to those who *fear God*. For years Lisa and I have endured lies, slander, accusations, and threats against us. I've jested with friends, "Don't google my name; you'll be inundated with articles denouncing me." But we've made it a point to keep silent and not defend ourselves. Instead, we've committed the attacks to the One we fear and have witnessed His constant protection. It hasn't been easy; there have been times I've literally cupped my hands and lifted them in the air as an outward sign of giving the accusations or threats to God. I cry out, "Father, I commit this into Your hands, please protect us." He's never failed us.

We've witnessed holy fear's protection for so many we know. Several years ago, I spoke to 1,500 people in our hometown. In the service many traded their fears for the fear of the Lord. The next evening, when a mother and daughter who were among those who had responded and were set free from fear returned to their home after shopping, they were met by three men with knives and guns. The men sternly ordered them into the house. Most likely their intent was to steal, rape, and possibly murder the two ladies.

The mother later reported, "Had it not been for the night before, I would have been frozen with fear, speechless, and complied with their demands." But she said, "I ignored their order to move into the house and instantly started praying aloud for Jesus to rescue us. My confidence, strength, and peace grew the more I cried out.

"The men started shaking, and they firmly ordered me to stop praying. Their patience eventually waned, and in a rage they started yelling, 'Stop, stop, stop this praying!'" The three men were unprepared to meet such confident women. The assailants were confused, and while they focused on the mother, the daughter was able to slip into the house to call for help. When the men suddenly realized she was missing, they fled.

That same year, as I was ministering in Houston, Texas, another young woman traded her fears for holy fear. Within a week of the service, after she came out of a shopping mall and got into her car, she discovered a man hiding in her back seat with a knife. He sternly commanded her to drive. Rather than being overwhelmed with fear, she cried out to Jesus and wouldn't stop. They drove for hours with the man demanding her to shut up, but she refused. He finally said, "Pull over!" and when she did, he opened the back door and fled.

There was a time when the king of Aram became furious with Elisha the prophet and sent troops to arrest him. Elisha's servant was the first to see the soldiers, horses, and chariots. He was overwhelmed with fear.

"'Don't be afraid!' Elisha told him. 'For there are *more on our side* than on theirs!' Then Elisha prayed, 'Oh LORD, open his eyes and let him see!'" (2 Kings 6:16–17). The Lord did, and the servant saw on the hillside multitudes of angelic horses and chariots of fire.

Jesus often encountered crowds that picked up stones to hurl at Him. Another time a crowd attempted to throw Him off a cliff, but in each life-threatening occasion, He simply walked away unharmed (see Luke 4:29; John 8:59, 10:39).

The only time God permits someone who fears Him to go through suffering is if it's granted from above for God's glory. However, even in these situations there is a confidence from holy fear that eliminates human fear. Consider the three young Hebrew men who were brought before the most powerful king on earth, King Nebuchadnezzar of Babylon. He had built a large idol and made a decree that all people should bow before it anytime music was heard in the land.

These three young men feared God and refused to sin by obeying the leader's decree. They were brought before a very angry Nebuchadnezzar, one who could instantly throw them into a furnace of fire. Were the young men afraid? I'll let you determine, for notice what they say to an enraged king: "If we are thrown into the blazing furnace, the God whom we serve is able to save us. He will rescue us from your power, Your Majesty. But even if he doesn't, we want to make it clear to you, Your Majesty, that we will never serve your gods or worship the gold statue you have set up" (Daniel 3:17–18).

What confidence! They remained calm and fearless, even though Scripture states, "Nebuchadnezzar was so furious with Shadrach, Meshach, and Abednego that his face became distorted with rage" (v. 19). These men feared God and therefore knew He would deliver them either by life or death. They were hurled into the furnace but came out unharmed, without even the smell of smoke. They remained unafraid, even if it meant death.

The apostle Paul, a man who greatly feared God, had the same attitude. When facing possible execution he stated, "I trust that my life will bring honor to Christ, whether I live or die. For to me, living means living for Christ, and dying is even better" (Philippians 1:20–21). Why is dying to glorify Christ even better or, as other translations say, "far better" than life? The fear of God, which is the beginning of wisdom, enlightens us with the proper perspective on this life and the next. This is why Jesus states, "Don't be afraid of those who want to kill your body; they cannot touch your soul. Fear only God, who can destroy both soul and body in hell" (Matthew 10:28).

Years ago, while I was on the road ministering, God spoke to me when I was fearful for my children. He said, "John, any fear in your life only identifies what you haven't put under the cross; you still own that area of your life." I repented that evening, gave our sons completely back to God, and never worried again for their safety. The fear of the Lord leads us to surrender all to Jesus. When we do, we live in what others greatly desire but just can't find: peace, confidence, and freedom from fear.

═══ **Making It Personal** ═══

Passage: Fear of the LORD leads to life, bringing security and protection from harm. (Proverbs 19:23)

Point: Any unbeneficial fear in your life only identifies what you haven't put under the cross; you still own that area of your life.

Ponder: In what areas of life do I battle fear? Is it my health, finances, marriage, children, job, schooling, being rejected, persecution for my faith, or another facet of my life? Have I completely given this area of my life to the lordship of Jesus, or do I still own it?

Prayer: Dear Lord, forgive me for not committing *(state whatever applies)* to You. In pondering, it's become clear that I've kept ownership of this. My insecurity has exposed the lack of holy fear in this area of my life. I repent and commit *(state whatever applies)*, and every area of my life, to the lordship of Jesus. Amen.

Profession: Jesus is my Lord. I give Him ownership of all areas of my life. May it be done unto me according to His will.

Direct your children onto the right path, and when they are older, they will not leave it.

—PROVERBS 22:6

38 | LEGACY

There is yet another great benefit of holy fear: godly legacy. Let me ask you some questions. What comes to mind when you think of Benedict Arnold? Is "traitor" your first thought? How about Mother Teresa? Do you think of Missionaries of Charity? How about Adolf Hitler? Do you think "tyrant dictator who murdered millions"? What about Albert Einstein? Do you think of the one who discovered the theory of relativity?

The thoughts that came to your mind are likely the legacies of these well-known individuals. The fact is, we all create legacies. So one question we need to ask ourselves is, will my legacy be well remembered or frowned upon? The bigger question, though, is how our legacy will be viewed in heaven—as beneficial or detrimental to the building of God's eternal kingdom.

One definition of the word *legacy*, according to Merriam-Webster, is "something transmitted by or received from an ancestor or predecessor."[1] How does the fear of God affect our posterity? To begin, let's return to the father of faith, Abraham. On the mountain, once the angel halted him from killing Isaac with the knife, the Lord said to him:

> *Blessing* I will *bless* you, and *multiplying* I will *multiply* your descendants . . . and your descendants shall possess the gate of their enemies. (Genesis 22:17 NKJV)

I've read these words for years and wondered why there are double references. Finally, my curiosity got the best of me, so I reached out to inquire of a rabbi, who replied: "In Jewish understanding when you have a double reference like this, it's all about multiplying . . . and because one verb tense is present tense and the other verb tense is future tense, it's described as one blessing on father Abraham, but God is promising that there will be blessings on his descendants. In other words, in blessing you, Abraham, I will continue to bless you through your children."

Holy fear benefits our descendants—"They will possess the gates of their enemies." This is wonderful, and we'll discuss it in a moment, but first there's another truth that should be highlighted from the rabbi's explanation. Holy fear continues to bless us through our descendants, and this is true not only in this life, but eternally.

Our forever is affected by our descendants creating greater honor and influence for us in both our near future and in the next life. To clarify, let me give an example. Archie Manning was an NFL quarterback for the New Orleans Saints for ten seasons. The team under his offensive leadership only made it to .500 once; the other nine seasons were losing seasons. He would have been forgotten by most, but two of his sons, Peyton and Eli, have won a combined four Super Bowls and were Super Bowl and league MVPs. Now more people know Archie due to his sons, and consequently he receives greater honor and influence in the world of sports.

In eternity, many will possess greater honor and influence due to their descendants' obedience in building the kingdom. Abraham is an excellent example; his eternal influence will be enhanced by his offspring—Joseph, Samuel, David, Daniel, Isaiah, and of course Jesus, just to name a few. Even now, his legacy continues. This blessing applies to all who fear God; they "will be long remembered" and "have influence and honor" (Psalm 112:6, 9). Many think everything starts over in heaven. However, this isn't true. As believers, we've already begun to shape eternal history, for we are told, "Their good deeds will be remembered forever" (Psalm 112:9).

Now let's turn to God's promise that our descendants will be conquerors; they will "possess the gate of their enemies." In a more contemporary vernacular, it could be stated that our offspring will not be overcome by those who despise God but instead will be successful leaders and influencers (Deuteronomy 28:13). You may think this is only for Abraham and his direct descendants. But we are told, "Through Christ Jesus, God has blessed the Gentiles with the same blessing he promised to Abraham" (Galatians 3:14). This is wonderful news!

> How joyful are those who fear the LORD and delight in obeying his commands. Their children will be successful everywhere; an entire *generation* of godly people will be blessed. (Psalm 112:1–2)

The word *generation* means "a long time,"[2] and it refers to our posterity.[3] Zechariah prophesied, "His mercy is on those who *fear Him* from generation to generation" (Luke 1:50 NKJV). Not only will our immediate children be successful, but this promise encompasses generations. A great example of this is found in the lives of two men, both born early in the eighteenth century.

The first is Max Jukes. In 1874 a sociologist named Richard Dugdale visited thirteen county jails in upstate New York. He discovered six persons under four different family names that were blood relatives. This sparked curiosity and led him into a deep dive of the family line. It led back to an early Dutch settler named Max Jukes, who was born somewhere between 1720 and 1740. After years of diligent research, Dugdale identified 540 descendants of Jukes. Among them were 76 convicted criminals, 18 brothel keepers, 120 prostitutes, and over 200 government-relief recipients. In short, there were generational sins that led to an abundance of dysfunctional behavior and cost the government tens of millions of dollars in today's currency value.[4]

Now let's compare him with Jonathan Edwards, who was born during the same time period. He was a revivalist who authored numerous books and inspired many to take the gospel to the nations. He was married to Sarah Pierpont in 1727. This couple greatly feared God. They read the Bible and prayed together every night before retreating. They had eleven children, and Jonathan prayed a blessing over each child daily. He stated, "Every house should be a little church."

Jonathan and Sarah's 1,394 known descendants reveal God's promise to those who fear Him—that they will *possess the gates of their enemies* and *their children will be successful everywhere*. Among their descendants are 13 college or university presidents, 65 college or university professors, 3 United States senators, 30 judges, 100 lawyers, 60 physicians, 75 army and navy officers, 100 ministers and missionaries, 60 authors of prominence, and 1 vice president of the United States, Aaron Burr. Their offspring didn't cost the government one penny.[5]

The fears I battled when our four sons were small children centered around their lives ending early, whether they would resent their dad being on the road preaching for sometimes over 200 nights a year, or that they would resent God for calling me to this. One evening, just after ministering at a conference far from home, I realized my lack of holy fear was preventing me from relinquishing ownership of their lives to Jesus. I shouted in prayer, "Father, these four sons are not mine anymore; they now belong to Jesus. You can do whatever you desire with them, but devil, you will never touch them!" Since that day, I've not feared for their lives.

Soon afterward God revealed a significant truth to me through His Word. Phinehas was a grandson to Aaron the priest. He was passionate for God and the people of Israel. His strong holy fear led him to do what other believers cowered from; he boldly stood for what was right. In doing so, God said, "Now tell him that I am making my special covenant of peace with him. In this covenant, I give him *and his descendants* a permanent right to the priesthood" (Numbers 25:12). In essence, his descendants were promised a more intimate relationship with God due to his holy fear. The Holy Spirit showed me that the protection for our sons was in Lisa's and my fervent obedience to His will.

Now, years later, each of our four sons has worked at Messenger International for at least nine years. Two are published authors, they all are leaders, and most importantly, they all walk in the holy fear of God. People constantly ask what we did to raise godly men. Honestly, it had nothing to do with our wisdom, and our many mistakes as parents could fill volumes of books. However, what we did do right is walk in a high level of holy fear.

When our sons went wayward for short stints during their teenage years, Lisa and I cried out to the Lord for His promise to be established in our sons, and we continued to live in holy fear. We never lost faith, and neither should you. God's promise to you who fear the Lord is that your children "will be mighty on earth" (Psalm 112:2 NKJV).

Making It Personal

Passage: Your children will be like vigorous young olive trees as they sit around your table. That is the LORD's blessing for those who fear him. (Psalm 128:3–4)

Point: When you abide in holy fear, something significant is transmitted to your descendants. Not only will they be influencers, but you will continue to be blessed through them.

Ponder: How do I view my children (or future children)? Do I worry about their future? Have I given them completely to the lordship of Jesus? Do I walk in holy fear before them? Do I perceive, pray, and speak according to their current behavior or what God's Word promises?

Prayer: Dear Lord, Your Word states that I will secure an enduring legacy by walking in holy fear. I believe Your promise that my children will be mighty on the earth, they will be influential, successful, and will bring honor to Your name and mine. I commit to continue to boldly pray for these promises to hold true. I ask this in Jesus' name, amen.

Profession: My children are mighty on the earth, successful everywhere they go, and they possess the gates of their enemies.

When we are defining in what man's true wisdom consists, the most convenient word to use is that which distinctly expresses the fear of God.

—AUGUSTINE OF HIPPO

39 | THE MOST IMPORTANT THING

The topic in this chapter is so vast that an entire book could be written on it alone. Yet to avoid it would make this message incomplete. So approach this chapter as an introduction to this important aspect of holy fear.

Listen to these words from our Creator's heart—words of life, words of truth, words that protect, words that will endure beyond the sun, moon, and stars, words surer than the earth we stand upon:

> Joyful is the person who finds wisdom, the one who gains understanding . . . *nothing* you desire can compare with her. (Proverbs 3:13, 15)

There is *nothing* in this world that equals the value of godly wisdom. It's remarkable—*nothing*! This is why we are told, "Getting wisdom is the most important thing you can do" (Proverbs 4:7 GNT)—and once found, it "will guide you down delightful paths; all her ways are satisfying" (Proverbs 3:17).

We should seek God's wisdom in every decision we make. For we are told: "If you prize wisdom, she will make you *great*" (Proverbs 4:8). What a magnificent promise! The Hebrew word for *great* is defined, "to raise, to lift up; to be exalted." When God promotes, no one and no circumstance can demote! Wisdom, therefore, is the path to enduring significance.

Wisdom must be discovered; it's hidden, but not out of reach. Once found, it brings tremendous benefits. So how do we find it?

The fear of the LORD is the *beginning* of wisdom. (Psalm 111:10; Proverbs 9:10 NKJV)

The Hebrew word for *beginning* is significant. It's found in the first verse of the Bible, "In the *beginning* God created the heavens and the earth." This word means "the starting place." Holy fear is the *originating point* for wisdom. Picture it like this: Consider a storehouse full of all the wisdom you need for enduring success. However, there's only one door and one key that can gain you access: holy fear. Isaiah writes, "A rich store of . . . wisdom and knowledge; the fear of the LORD is *the key* to this treasure" (Isaiah 33:6 NIV).

In essence, there is no lasting wisdom outside of the fear of the Lord. Holy fear is the origin of enduring wisdom, but the benefit continues beyond the starting place:

The fear of the LORD is a *fountain* of life, to turn one away from the *snares* of death. (Proverbs 14:27 NKJV)

I want to highlight two key words: *fountain* and *snares*. The Hebrew word for *fountain* carries the meaning of "a flow" or a constant source. To live well doesn't result from sporadic good decisions, rather from a consistent flow of wise decisions that bear lasting fruit.

The second word, *snares*, refers to traps or bait. "The proper understanding of this Hebrew word is the lure or bait placed in a hunter's trap."[1] Any good hunter knows that a trap needs two things to be successful. It must be hidden, in hopes that the animal will not recognize it for what it is, and it must be baited to entice the animal into the trap's deadly jaws. With a good understanding of the key words, look at another passage that offers greater clarity to the truth being stated:

The fear of the LORD is the *instruction of wisdom.* (Proverbs 15:33 NKJV)

In combining the truths of these two passages, we discover that holy fear is a fountain—a continual flow—of the instruction of God's wisdom. It's an ever-present counselor that doesn't slumber or sleep but consistently coaches us to make wise decisions in life.

When we are left on our own, separate from God's wisdom, mankind has proven for thousands of years that we will make detrimental decisions all the while thinking we're making good ones. Why is this? The ways of death and destruction are hidden and baited, no different from a hunter's trap. What appears to be good, wise, beneficial, and enjoyable is often merely bait to lure you into what ultimately is bad, unwise, detrimental, and grieving. The fear of the Lord protects us from this by *faithfully turning us away from these traps.*

If you look at today's society, we have great and intelligent men and women making decisions that are steering those they influence into ruin. At the same time others are blind to their foolishness. Scripture states that in rejecting holy fear, "their minds became dark and confused. Claiming to be wise, they instead became utter fools" (Romans 1:21–22). When minds are darkened, vision is also darkened; it's only a matter of time before we fall headlong into death's hidden and baited traps.

However, the flip side is also true. When we firmly embrace holy fear, we have an ever-present, constant-flowing counselor of wisdom that gives us the ability to make enduring beneficial decisions. Even when we are unaware of lurking death traps, the fountain continually protects us from unknowingly becoming ensnared.

Let's look at this principle as we examine a man who didn't have a covenant with God yet feared Him. It was King Abimelech of Gerar. He had taken Abraham's wife, Sarah, into his harem. Soon afterward, God comes to him at night and says, "You are a dead man, for the woman you have taken is already married!" (Genesis 20:3).

Abimelech cries out, "Lord . . . I acted in complete innocence! My hands are clean" (vv. 4–5). In regard to the word used here for "Lord," we are told, "this word means literally 'my Lord.'"[2] His fear of God is quite evident in the way he addresses God as well as his response. Now listen to what God says to him,

> "Yes, I know you are innocent. That's why I *kept you from sinning against me*, and why I did not let you touch her." (Genesis 20:6)

The fear of the Lord was a counselor, one he was unaware of, to keep him from falling into the snare of death. The trap was hidden due to the deceptive way she was presented—as being Abraham's sister—yet holy fear protected him. How is it that this pagan king, who had no known covenant with God, who did not have the written word of God, trembled at the thought of taking another man's wife? We find our answer in Paul's writings: "Even Gentiles, who do not have God's written law, show that they know his law when they instinctively obey it, even without having heard it. They demonstrate that God's law is written in their hearts, for their own conscience and thoughts either accuse them or tell them they are doing right" (Romans 2:14–15).

Furthermore, how is it this Gentile king trembles at the thought of taking another man's wife, yet a seasoned pastor or one who has attended church for years takes another man's wife in adultery, something we are witnessing more frequently as time passes? It's not rocket science. Even though this church leader or attender confesses with his mouth to belong to Jesus, he has no fear of God. We are told:

> I find more bitter than death the woman whose heart *is* snares and nets, whose hands are fetters. He who pleases God shall escape from her, but the *sinner* shall be trapped by her. (Ecclesiastes 7:26 NKJV)

Scripture doesn't say the *wicked* shall be trapped, but the *sinner*—one who is missing the mark due to his lack of holy fear. This can easily be someone who professes Christianity. James writes to professing believers, "Wash your hands, you *sinners*; purify your hearts, for your loyalty is divided between God and the world" (James 4:8).

Our broadly accepted Western gospel has systematically removed the fear of God from our hearts by teaching a *counterfeit* grace that trains us differently than God's wisdom. It creates an unhealthy fountain of perverted counsel that removes the restraining force protecting us from sin. However, authentic grace doesn't conflict with holy fear.

> For the grace of God that brings salvation has appeared to all men, *teaching us* that, denying ungodliness and worldly lusts, we should live soberly, righteously, and godly in the present age. (Titus 2:11–12 NKJV)

We cannot separate the true grace of God from the holy fear of God. They are united and both *teach*—continually counsel us away from the traps of death.

This plague of ungodly behavior among professing covenant people is nothing new. All through Israel's and the church's history we've seen the same pattern, but it's intensified during these latter days that Jesus said would be marked by deception. The loss of holy fear opens people's hearts and souls to dark counsel, appearing to be truth, when in reality, it unknowingly leads to sin and death.

Presently, in our society, the force of lawlessness is on an accelerated pace. It's as if were on the upswing of an exponential curve. If the widely accepted counterfeit grace continues to eliminate holy fear from believers' hearts, multitudes of professing Christians will be swept away by lawlessness's deception. We need a revival of holy fear, for it continually protects us from being fooled. It keeps our hearts in line with truth, even when the majority have fallen headlong into deception.

Embrace holy fear as your great treasure. Guard it more diligently than you would millions of dollars, the most expensive jewelry, or the nicest home. We protect these valuables in federally insured banks, vaults, safes, or by installing alarm systems, yet our greatest treasure is the fear of the Lord.

This is why we are told, "Guard your heart above all else, for it determines the course of your life" (Proverbs 4:23).

══════════ **Making It Personal** ══════════

Passage: Listen as Wisdom calls out! Hear as understanding raises her voice! . . . For whoever finds me finds life and receives favor from the LORD. But those who miss me injure themselves. (Proverbs 8:1, 35–36)

Point: As a Christ follower, getting wisdom is the most important thing we can do. The fear of the Lord is the fountain of wisdom; it protects us from the traps of death.

Ponder: Have I drawn a line in the sand? Have I determined to not adhere to the wisdom of society that is contrary to what the Word of God states? Am I willing to be persecuted for my belief in and obedience to His Word? How will I seek Jesus' wisdom more carefully in my daily decisions?

Prayer: Dear Father, in the name of Jesus, I cry out for Your wisdom and understanding. Please open my ears and eyes to perceive it. I don't want to be a fool by being wise in my own opinions. I will prize and depend on the wisdom of my Lord Jesus Christ above anything this world has to offer. I choose to obey even if I'm persecuted for my beliefs or obedience. Amen.

Profession: I am determined to seek my Lord Jesus' wisdom in every decision I make.

The fear of God corresponds to the humble.

—AUGUSTINE OF HIPPO

40 | SUCCESSFUL LIVING

Deep in the wisdom of the book of Proverbs there are what I like to call "the power twins." These two virtues go hand in hand, often complementing each other in Scripture. They are identified in the following verse:

> *True humility* and *fear of the* LORD lead to riches, honor, and long life.
> (Proverbs 22:4)

True humility and holy fear are connected. You will never find someone who fears God who is not truly humble, nor will you find anyone who is truly humble who doesn't fear God. The word "truly" is important, as there are various forms of counterfeit humility. We'll address this more thoroughly in the next chapter.

Let's briefly look at the three listed promises: riches, honor, and long life. The Hebrew word for "riches" is *ʿōšer*, and is defined as "Wealth, riches. It describes all kinds of wealth in land, possessions, cattle, and descendants." Its meaning is clear, and it's not a one-time promise regarding holy fear. The psalmist also writes:

> How joyful are those who fear the Lord and delight in obeying his com-
> mands. . . . They themselves will be *wealthy*, and their good deeds will last
> forever. (Psalm 112:1, 3)

It's the same Hebrew word for wealthy, *ōšer*. This presents a potential
controversy. There are some who view possessing riches and wealth as being
contrary to godliness. However, if we eliminate clear scriptural truths for
the sake of our tradition, isn't it an indicator of pride, which is certainly the
antithesis of holy fear?

I had to come to grips with this years ago. In our early years of ministry,
Lisa and I witnessed ministers teaching a prosperity gospel that led many to
chase after decadent opulence. The fruit was devastating, leading many into
covetousness, which is idolatry. A good number wandered from the true
faith and brought on themselves various sorrows. In witnessing the casualties, we responded by swinging the pendulum the opposite direction. We
grew to disdain any teaching that mentioned wealth, riches, or prosperity.
Our immaturity was eventually corrected by the Holy Spirit. We had to face
the truth that a person who truly fears God will handle wealth properly and
not succumb to the trap of covetousness.

What is the purpose of wealth and riches? They are a means for blessing
others. At the time of this writing, our ministry has given over 53 million
physical resources—books and courses—to pastors and leaders in 130
nations in 118 languages. We've also created an app, called MessengerX,
that's loaded with discipleship resources in 122 languages that has been
downloaded in 230 nations; we've not charged for its use. These projects
have cost tens of millions of dollars. What if the men and women who've
supported these efforts believed that godliness is synonymous with lack or
poverty? If they did, we wouldn't have strengthened the multiple millions
who've been reached.

There is a huge difference between covetousness and possessing
wealth to impact lives. Those who truly fear God know the difference and
stay clear of the former. In the New Testament, after Jesus was crucified,
we read:

Now when evening had come, there came a *rich* man from Arimathea, named Joseph, who himself had also become a *disciple of Jesus*. This man went to Pilate and asked for the body of Jesus. (Matthew 27:57–58 NKJV)

Joseph was wealthy, and Scripture calls him a disciple of Jesus. However, the irony continues—most of Jesus' followers had fled and hidden. Yet this rich man has the boldness, which stemmed from his holy fear, to ignore the intimidation of the Jewish leaders and the might of Rome, and approach Pilate to ask for the body of Jesus. What a brave man!

Please don't misunderstand. If someone is poor, does it mean they lack the fear of God? No! Scripture is loaded with men and women who didn't possess material wealth. Did it make them less godly? Absolutely not! True wealth is not measured in money or possessions but in our ability to help others. Here is our promise:

Fear the LORD, you his godly people, for those who fear him will have all they need. Even strong young lions sometimes go hungry, but those who trust in the LORD will lack no good thing. (Psalm 34:9–10)

It's a godly desire to impact others for the kingdom, whether it's prayer, food, finances, teaching, discipling, hospitality, or serving. It's good to have an abundance of resources for accomplishing whatever is needed for our divine mission. Godly people pursue this and, in the process, find themselves personally blessed. The proud, religious, and envious will spend their energies arguing why believers should be poor and hold people to convictions that aren't founded in Scripture.

King Solomon led and taught the people of his kingdom in the fear of the Lord. During this time, "all of Judah and Israel lived in peace and safety. And from Dan to the north to Beersheba in the south, *each family* had its *own home* and *garden*" (1 Kings 4:25). We are further told the people "were very contented, with *plenty* to eat and drink" (1 Kings 4:20). Stop and consider the statement, "*each family* had its own home and garden." There was no welfare, unemployment, or poverty with anyone in the entire nation—everyone had plenty! The fear of the Lord gives the wisdom that benefits all those under its influence; in this case it was an entire nation. What would happen if all our leaders walked in the fear of the Lord?

As a final thought, this promise isn't one we have to fight for in prayer, as Isaac had to contend for Rebekah's womb to open. Jesus promises us, "Seek the Kingdom of God above all else, and live righteously, and he will give you everything you need" (Matthew 6:33).

Let's look at the next promise, *honor*. The Hebrew word for "honor" in our opening verse is *kāḇôḏ* and is defined as "honor, glory, majesty, wealth." We saw in an earlier chapter that this is the word Moses used when requesting to see God's glory. It carries a weightiness, an authority not stemming from a title or position, but rather attached to character. So we discover yet another wonderful benefit of holy fear: nobility. It transforms you into a person of dignity and honor. Proverbs isn't the only book stating this benefit; the psalmist uses the same Hebrew word for those who fear God: "They will have influence and *honor*" (Psalm 112:9).

Consider the virtuous woman in the book of Proverbs. She possesses tremendous qualities. She's trustworthy, wise, diligent, energetic, hard-working, prosperous, wealthy, kind, assists those in need, and defends the helpless. Another outstanding trait that is sometimes overlooked and is pertinent to our discussion is, "She is clothed with strength and dignity" (Proverbs 31:25). In other words, she wears honor like a garment, no different from our clothing—it's visible and noticeable to all in her presence. And what is her final virtue?

> Charm is deceptive, and beauty does not last; but a woman who *fears the* LORD will be greatly praised. (Proverbs 31:30)

It's holy fear! Here is the amazing reality—the nobility and dignity ascribed to this woman are available to any man or woman who fears God. In all my years of traveling I've met many significant leaders and individuals. Many have greatly impacted society, but what grabs my attention more than anything they've built is when I encounter a man or woman who wears dignity. There's a weightiness to their presence. They radiate light, love, honor, and nobility. Their children love and respect them, and their coworkers and friends love being in close proximity. Interestingly, a good number of them are not public figures. What's their calling card? They fear God!

The third promise in our opening verse is *long life*, or longevity. It's closely tied to true humility. We'll expand on this promise in our next chapter.

Making It Personal

Passage: All who fear the LORD will hate evil . . . I love all who love me. Those who search will surely find me. I have riches and honor, as well as enduring wealth and justice. (Proverbs 8:13, 17–18)

Point: Holy fear and humility promise riches, honor, and long life. Wealth is not measured by the amount of money or possessions we have but by our ability to help others. Nobility is wrapped up in our character, not our title or position.

Ponder: Do I view wealth in a healthy light? Do I pursue it out of insecurity, fear, or covetousness? Would I be better off to pursue holy fear and believe the promise to have an abundance to impact others? What does it mean for me to be clothed with dignity?

Prayer: Dear Father, please fulfill Your promise that in my pursuit of true humility and holy fear I will experience the wealth, honor, and long life needed to fulfill my divine mission of serving others. In Jesus' name, amen.

Profession: I have been promised by my heavenly Father riches, honor, and a long life in pursuing holy fear and true humility.

A sensible person stays
on the right path.

—PROVERBS 15:21

41 | FINISHING WELL

We cannot fully discuss living well unless we include finishing well. In the chapter 18 we touched on longevity, but in this chapter we'll expound further and examine how the fear of the Lord and humility play an important role.

> True humility and fear of the LORD lead to riches, honor, and *long life*.
> (Proverbs 22:4)

A fabulous benefit of holy fear is prolonged days. We read: "Fear of the LORD lengthens one's life" (Proverbs 10:27). What a promise! And it's not a one-time occurrence, for again we are told the wisdom of holy fear will "multiply your days and add years to your life" (Proverbs 9:11). Not only are we promised added years but that our days will be more productive.

Still another confirmation is found in one of the Ten Commandments. The fear of the Lord inspires us to unconditionally honor our parents, and in so doing we are promised that "things will go well for you, and you will have a long life on the earth" (Ephesians 6:3). Once again, we find not only longevity but also productivity. These are promises we can ask for in prayer.

With this said, it's important to note that without quality of life, the pleasure of added years diminishes. Solomon wrote in his pessimistic years, "The day you die is better than the day you are born" (Ecclesiastes 7:1). It's obvious he must not have been enjoying life when he penned these words. What ensures quality of life? True humility and the fear of the Lord.

Years ago, I was in prayer and read:

> In the year that King Uzziah died, I saw the Lord sitting on a throne, high and lifted up, and the train of His *robe* filled the temple. (Isaiah 6:1 NKJV)

Isaiah saw the Lord in all His glory. As discussed in an earlier chapter, he beheld the Almighty on His throne, the massive angels, and the doorposts of the building shaking from their cries. From this experience, his life was radically transformed.

After reading the account, I cried out, "Lord, this is what I need, a fresh vision of Jesus!"

The Holy Spirit whispered to my heart, "That's not how I started the verse. Go back and read it again."

I was perplexed, yet I did as He instructed, and this time the words "In the year that King Uzziah died" leapt off the page.

Then I heard, "Uzziah had to die before Isaiah could have a fresh vision of Me."

At the time, I wasn't familiar with Uzziah; I just knew he was one of the many kings of either Israel or Judah. But when I started researching his life, I discovered some fascinating realities. He was only sixteen years old when he was crowned king of Judah, and he reigned fifty-two years. For perspective, at the time of this writing, I've been under ten United States presidents in the past fifty-two years. Uzziah reigned for quite some time.

In being handed rulership over millions of people at the age of sixteen, he did the wise thing—he sought God. We read, "As long as he sought the LORD, God made him prosper" (2 Chronicles 26:5 NKJV). Wow, did he succeed! The wisdom God gave him propelled him to startling greatness. He strengthened the economy, restored cities, built a mighty military, and took back territories that were lost by his fathers. We read, "His fame spread far

and wide, for the LORD gave him marvelous help, and he became very powerful" (2 Chronicles 26:15).

However, as with Solomon, the fear of the Lord wasn't his treasure.
Tragically, we read:

> But when he had become powerful, he also became *proud*, which led to his
> downfall. (2 Chronicles 26:16)

Somewhere along the line he lost the humility and holy fear he began
with. Here's an important truth: these power-twin virtues will produce a
momentum of fruitfulness, which means the success will usually continue
even when the virtues that initiated and propelled it are no longer behind it.
What we read next is quite interesting:

> He sinned against the LORD his God by entering the sanctuary of the
> LORD's Temple and personally burning incense on the incense altar.
> (2 Chronicles 26:16)

The Holy Spirit asked me a question: "Son, did Uzziah become *more*
spiritual or *less* spiritual when pride entered his heart?" I realized immediately that the answer was counterintuitive. I had always thought when pride
enters the heart of someone, they become less spiritual. However, Uzziah
entered the temple to do a spiritual activity before the Lord. I wouldn't have
recognized this unless the Holy Spirit had asked the question.

In shock, I blurted out loud, "He became *more* spiritual!"

The Holy Spirit whispered to my heart, "A spirit of pride and a spirit of
religion go hand in hand, and they strengthen each other by hiding each
other." Pride keeps a person from admitting they've become religious, and
religion covers up the pride by its spiritual behavior.

I then thought of the Pharisees of Jesus' day. Similar to Uzziah, these
leaders probably started out with a genuine love and holy fear for Jehovah,
but at some point, pride entered their hearts. They grew more distant from
God, but their involvement in spiritual activities intensified.

Uzziah was confronted by the priests; they called out his unscriptural behavior. When challenged with truth, Uzziah became furious with the priests (also an indicator of a loss of humility). Suddenly, leprosy broke out on his forehead. The remainder of this king's life was tragic; he had to live in an isolated house. His son took over his rule of the royal palace, and eventually Uzziah died with leprosy.

Let's view this through the general public's eye. The only evident reality to the people of Judah and Jerusalem was that their king contracted leprosy. Can you imagine how social media would blow up? Comments flooding the networks: "Oh no! Our king's got leprosy; what a tragedy!" None of the people knew what was behind the disease. But we are given the inside scoop by the Holy Spirit—it was a loss of holy fear and humility.

In seeing this, I further inquired of the Lord in regard to our day. My heart has broken over the numerous leaders in my lifetime who've fallen. Most often it's an extramarital affair, but sometimes it's through alcoholism, drug addiction, greed, or other vices and inappropriate behaviors. I've sadly watched leaders fall who started in ministry before us, at the same time, and even after us. Every one of them began with a great zeal to glorify Jesus. How could they succumb to such dark behavior? Didn't they see others follow the same pattern?

The Holy Spirit again spoke to me: "Son, these fallen leaders didn't have a hormone problem, they had a pride problem." What all of us witnessed is the leprosy breaking out on their foreheads—their affairs, vices, or other behavior that led to their downfall. What we didn't see is the pride that replaced their holy fear and humility. At what point this occurs, only God knows. Not even the leader knows, because pride blinds its victim from seeing clearly.

Due to the momentum that success creates, we can easily lose sight of what got us there—diligently seeking God with humility and holy fear. This is why it is utterly important that in our times of success we keep before us Jesus' words: "Apart from me you can do nothing" (John 15:5).

In essence, the Holy Spirit said to me that day, "John, to the degree pride dies is the degree you will have a fresh vision of Jesus." Transformation is imperative, and without a fresh vision of Him, we miss the opportunity to grow more like Him. Many great men and women have not finished well, yet all of them believed they could escape the inevitable consequence of a loss of humility and holy fear. Don't be fooled—cling tight to true humility, your utter dependence on Jesus, and make holy fear your treasure. Do this and God promises riches, honor, and long life.

Making It Personal

Passage: Listen to me and do as I say, and you will have a long, good life. (Proverbs 4:10)

Point: To the degree pride dies is the degree we will have a fresh vision of Jesus. True humility is rooted in holy fear. It's knowing that without Jesus, we can do nothing. Therefore, we choose to be completely and utterly dependent on Him.

Ponder: Is humility a reality in my life? Are there areas that I have the attitude, *I've got this*? Do I make plans without consulting the Lord? Do I make decisions without looking inside for His witness? If so, how can I change this approach? How does being thankful keep me both bold and humble?

Prayer: Dear Father, in Jesus' name, forgive me for pride in these areas of my life: (*list them*). I repent of this self-dependency and for esteeming myself above others. Cleanse me with the blood of Jesus. I humble myself in Your sight and in so doing choose to see others as more important than myself. Amen.

Profession: I choose humility and the fear of the Lord to guide my life.

I do pray often: "Oh God, send a revival of repentance and the fear of God that will sweep through the continent that we may be spared and that we may honor Thee!"

—A. W. TOZER

42 | FINDING THE TREASURE

(Note to the reader: This chapter will be longer than normal in order to complete the message properly. If you've been reading on a daily basis, I've broken this chapter up into two readings: morning and evening.)

Morning Reading: Summary of Benefits

The depth of the benefits holy fear provides are too numerous for one book. It would take volumes to thoroughly discuss them. I've been searching for almost three decades and am still in awe of what the Holy Spirit unfolds in Scripture. So let's wrap up this volume by briefly peeking at a few more promises. See each as an introduction to your further exploration and discovery. Embrace these promises in your heart. Do not attempt to write them off or explain them away. Speak them back to God. For those who fear God, these are your gems to find and lay hold of.

> How *joyful* are those who fear the LORD—all who follow his ways! You will *enjoy* the fruit of your labor. How *joyful* and prosperous you will be! (Psalm 128:1–2)

Notice the root word "joy" appears three times in just two verses! A person who truly fears God abounds with joy. One aspect of joy that's specifically stated is our labor. I will never forget a life-impacting incident that occurred when I was an engineer for IBM in the early 1980s. We were celebrating a fellow engineer's thirty-eight-year anniversary. There were a dozen of us huddled in his office at the start of our day.

At one point, the man we were celebrating blurted out, "I've hated every day I've walked into this facility for thirty-eight years." The others laughed and nodded in agreement.

I had only been working in my position for a few months; I was young and ignorant, but now confused. I questioned, "Why did you do it?"

His countenance quickly changed from a snicker to disgust as he turned to me, along with everyone else in the office, and sneered, "John, it's called a job! You have to work to buy food and clothing." By the looks on the other men's faces I could see they shared his sentiments. I knew not to say another word as I was not in the company of wise men.

The only reason I had studied engineering was the fear of not securing a well-paying job. His comment exposed my unholy fear. I determined that day that I would not be uttering the same words thirty-eight years later. This fear would not direct my life; I would trust God. I can happily say, since that time, I've enjoyed the fruit of my labor, and this promise is for all who fear God.

The psalmist continues:

Your wife will be like a fruitful grapevine, flourishing within your home. Your children will be like vigorous young olive trees as they sit around your table. *That is the* Lord's *blessing for those who fear him.* (Psalm 128: 3–4)

You'll enjoy the fruit of your work, your spouse will flourish, and your enthusiastic children will want to be in your company. Too many lack what's described in these passages; in fact, this identifies what's missing in the greater part of our society. So many, even if they make a lot of money, are not enjoying life. They don't get along with their spouses, and their children want nothing to do with the family. Their families are withering rather than flourishing—but there's a divine hope.

The hope of this promise is specific and most wonderful. It's not for all who attend church or even confess a relationship with Jesus. It explicitly states, "That is the LORD's blessing for those who fear him."

Dear reader, you've almost completed your journey through this message. By getting this far, you've chosen to fear God; therefore, it's a promise you can ask for in prayer. Cry out to God, just as Isaac did, to see these promises of holy fear fulfilled. We experienced extended months in which these promises weren't a reality in our household; there were indicators pointing they may not occur, but we held on to the hope of God's promises and contended for them in prayer. Now we can say for years they've been fulfilled in our family.

Let's turn to another psalm that speaks in depth of those who fear God:

> Praise the LORD! How *joyful* are those who fear the LORD and delight in
> obeying his commands. Their children will be successful everywhere; an
> entire generation of godly people will be blessed. (Psalm 112:1–2)

Once again, we see the word "joyful" connected with holy fear. Joy is a spiritual force; it is not founded in circumstance, as is happiness. Rather, joy is founded in the eternal Word of God; it's our strength. It makes us more productive and fruitful.

Also in this verse, we see that holy fear greatly affects our descendants. Not only will we be successful, but our children are promised the same. Let's continue:

> They themselves will be wealthy, and their good deeds will last forever. . . .
> Such people will not be overcome by evil. Those who are righteous will be
> long remembered. They do not fear bad news; they confidently trust the
> LORD to care for them. They are confident and fearless and can face their
> foes triumphantly. (Psalm 112:3, 6–8)

Recently, I was speaking with another believer, and she commented how one day, when we leave this life, our eternity will commence. I quickly countered, "No, for those of us who've been reborn, our eternity has already begun." Our present labor of love will continue forever. However, those who lack holy fear do not have this promise—in fact just the opposite: "Whatever they did in their lifetime—loving, hating, envying—is all long gone" (Ecclesiastes 9:6).

Those who fear God do not fear bad news. In this day of abundant social media, mainstream media, and the plethora of other news and gossip outlets, bad news is at an all-time high. So many are fearful of what's coming. But there's no dread or fear of the future for those who fear God; they are confident and fearless. Again, we are told:

> In the fear of the LORD *there is* strong confidence, and His children will have a place of refuge. (Proverbs 14:26 NKJV)

There is an inner confidence that accompanies holy fear. This is something many long for but soon discover that it seems out of reach. I have a friend, John Hagee, who is a highly respected pastor in Texas. He fears God as much as any leader I've ever met. In 1973 a man walked into his service and somehow got to within eight feet of him and unloaded six rounds from a .38 revolver. Pastor John stood confidently and didn't move. All six rounds missed him. At the time of this writing, he's alive fifty years later, still preaching the gospel. In this situation most would have lost any semblance of poise, screamed, and hit the deck or sought shelter. John didn't budge but confidently kept his gaze on the shooter. We are told:

> The angel of the LORD is a guard; he surrounds and defends all who fear him. (Psalm 34:7)

Angels are assigned to protect those who fear God. Forensics later determined half the bullets missed Pastor John six inches to the left of his body and the other half missed six inches to the right of his body. The shooter missed from eight feet! Even inexperienced gun handlers would hit the target from eight feet with six chances. We are confident that an angel of God redirected the bullets.

King Jehoshaphat of Judah was a man who was "deeply committed to the ways of the LORD" (2 Chronicles 17:6). In the third year of his reign, he sent out the priests to every town of his nation to teach the people the word of God. We read:

Then the fear of the LORD fell over all the surrounding kingdoms so that none of them wanted to declare war on Jehoshaphat. (2 Chronicles 17:10)

There is great protection in abiding in holy fear. Another biblical example is Jacob, who directed his family to fear God and to put away their idols. Once they did, we read, "As they set out, a terror from God spread over the people in all the towns of that area, so no one attacked Jacob's family" (Genesis 35:5).

Those who are devoted to fearing the Lord are promised so much. Look at these words:

Always continue to fear the LORD. You will be *rewarded* for this; your *hope* will not be disappointed. (Proverbs 23:17–18)

Notice the two highlighted words. First, in a day when *hope* is scarce, many spiritual leaders are making inspiration their main focus and conversely treating the Word of God as a sidebar. A scripture or two are spoken to appease the serious listeners, but the main thrust is their inspiring stories. Though these tales will benefit and move people in the short term—no different from an inspiring Hollywood movie—they will not have the promised enduring *rewards* of holy fear.

The fear of the Lord rewards us in so many ways: desires fulfilled (see Psalm 145:19), faithful friends (Psalm 119:63, 74, 79), healing for our bodies (Proverbs 3:7–8), identity (Psalm 60:4), and the direction in life so many are longing for.

Who are those who fear the Lord? He will show them the path they should choose. They will live in prosperity, and their children will inherit the land. (Psalm 25:12–13)

Why anyone would not treasure holy fear is beyond comprehension. It is my earnest desire that you will see its value and not keep it to yourself, but that you would be like King Jehoshaphat who taught all the people under his influence to fear God.

Evening Reading: Finding Holy Fear

The Lord spoke to me more than thirty years ago that the final move of God in this age would emphasize holy fear. The great benefit of this awakening would be the fulfillment of the single description in Scripture of the bride Jesus is returning for. She's not a "relevant" church, although relevance is important in reaching the lost. She's not a "leadership-driven" church, although leadership is crucial to building a strong church. She's not a "community church," although community is vital because it's not good for man to be alone. Here is the only description of the bride He's returning for:

He did this to present her to himself as a glorious church without a spot or wrinkle or any other blemish. Instead, she will be *holy* and without fault. (Ephesians 5:27)

It is a holy church! Dear reader, since holiness is perfected in the fear of God, it's our Lord's earnest desire for you to be an influencer in this great awakening. Therefore, it is important to finish our discussion with how to increase our holy fear.

Let me bring you back to the awesome and riveting service in Malaysia. During the manifestation of His majestic and mighty presence, I was trembling in awe and thinking to myself, *John Bevere, don't say one wrong word or make one wrong move.*

As I was pacing back and forth on the platform thinking this, something came out of my mouth that my ears heard for the first time after saying it. I had never thought of or considered this before. I boldly stated, "This is the Spirit of the fear of the Lord!"

Suddenly, lights went flashing off in my mind. I shouted within myself, *That's it, that's it—this is one of the manifestations of the Holy Spirit!* I had never put this together, but in Scripture we are told of Jesus:

> The Spirit of the LORD shall rest upon Him, the Spirit of wisdom and [the Spirit of] understanding, the Spirit of counsel and [the Spirit of might], the Spirit of knowledge and of the [Spirit of the] fear of the LORD. His delight is in the fear of the LORD. (Isaiah 11:2–3 NKJV)

There are seven listed ways the Holy Spirit manifests, and Jesus walked in the fullness of them all, but His delight was in holy fear. So the question becomes, how do we receive the *Spirit of the fear of the Lord?* Jesus tells us, "If you then, being evil, know how to give good gifts to your children, how much more will your heavenly Father give the Holy Spirit to those who ask Him!" (Luke 11:13 NKJV).

We simply need to ask our heavenly Father. However, it's not a casual ask, but a cry from our heart and one that refuses to take no for an answer. Just prior to these words He tells us, "Keep on asking, and you will receive what you ask for. Keep on seeking, and you will find" (Luke 11:9). There's a persistence highlighted here.

Let's go back to 1994, to the conference where the pastor corrected me for speaking on the fear of the Lord. The next morning at the construction site, I started praying in the direction of "what did I do wrong?" but ended up passionately crying loudly for holy fear. It was a determined request, one that wouldn't take no for an answer. At the time, I wasn't aware of the importance of the moment, but now I see it as one of the most crucial and

transforming events of my life. Even now, on almost a daily basis, I passionately ask my heavenly Father for a fresh infilling of the Holy Spirit of the fear
of the Lord. Let's look at another portion of Scripture that will carry great
relevance to our discussion.

> My child, listen to what I say, and treasure my commands. Tune your ears
> to wisdom, and concentrate on understanding. Cry out for insight, and
> ask for understanding. Search for them as you would for silver; seek them
> like hidden treasures. Then you will understand what it means to fear the
> LORD, and you will gain knowledge of God. (Proverbs 2:1–5)

There must be a deep cry coupled with a diligent search for holy fear, no
different than you would search for a misplaced diamond engagement ring
or lost gold jewelry. I'm sure you've watched programs or movies involving
treasure hunters, which always convey a sense of unrelenting persistence
on the searcher's part. One that stands out is the fictional movie *National
Treasure*[1]. Made in 2004, it depicts a man, Benjamin Gates, who spent his
life searching for a stockpile of treasure that was hidden away in the 1700s.
He gave all of his time and energy—even to the point of risking his reputation and his freedom—to find it. Though what he searched for will all perish
one day soon, his relentless persistence is what should inspire us.

If we would approach God's Word, His wisdom, divine counsel, and
holy fear with this same resolve, we would be most blessed. We are crying
out for what will never perish; it's God's treasure. He has not hidden it *from
us*, but *for us*. He's cheering us on to find it and rejoices when we do. He also
celebrates when we experience its rewards.

It's my earnest hope that by the help of the Holy Spirit, what was birthed
in me that morning at the construction site has been birthed in you—an
insatiable hunger for the fear of the Lord. Treasure it and hold on to it as if it
were your greatest asset. If you do, you'll love what God loves and hate what
He hates; what's important to Him will become what's important to you.
You'll deeply love people and deeply hate the sin that unmakes them. You'll
change your world of influence and be glad you did throughout eternity.

Please remember, *it's not how we start this race that's important, but how we finish it.* Two passages that give great hope and strength along these lines are:

Now all glory to God, who is able to *keep you from falling away* and will bring you with great joy into his glorious presence without a single fault. (Jude 24)

He will keep you *strong to the end* so that you will be free from all blame on the day when our Lord Jesus Christ returns. (1 Corinthians 1:8)

Finishing well is the most important aspect of living well, and God has granted us holy fear to accomplish it. It has been an honor to introduce you to this treasure. Please don't keep it to yourself; there's plenty to go around. Share this message with your world of influence. If you do, we'll see fewer casualties in the coming days and a healthier church.

Choose now to be a part of the mighty transformational move of holy fear that will prepare the bride for the return of our Groom. Don't be on the outside looking in. By embracing holy fear, you'll find deep intimacy with our Bridegroom, your salvation will be matured, you'll be very fruitful, and you will build an eternal legacy.

Making It Personal

Passage: Now to Him who is able to keep you from stumbling, and to present *you* faultless before the presence of His glory with exceeding joy, to God our Savior, Who alone is wise, be glory and majesty, dominion and power, both now and forever. Amen. (Jude 24–25 NKJV)

Point: Finishing well is the most important aspect of living well. God, through His gift of holy fear, will keep you strong and blameless to the end.

Ponder: What do I need to do to increase holy fear in my life? Do I long for and thus relentlessly pursue holy fear as a treasure? Will I hold on to it as one of my most prized possessions? What should I do on a regular basis to maintain it?

Prayer: Dear Father, I cry out to You to fill me with the Spirit of the Lord, the Spirit of wisdom, the Spirit of understanding, the Spirit of counsel, the Spirit of might, the Spirit of knowledge, and the Spirit of the fear of the Lord. Keep me strong to the end that I may be found blameless on the day of my Lord Jesus Christ. In Jesus' name I pray, amen.

Profession: The fear of the Lord is my treasure.

LINK TO VIDEOS AND OTHER BONUS CONTENT

Click on the QR code below for bonus content that includes:

- 42 short videos that highlight the core truths from each chapter, which will lead you on a deeper, more personal journey.
- Information on a study guide and video curriculum created especially for small groups to build community and strengthen the local church.
- Other material to show you how to receive the holy fear of the Lord.

A GLIMPSE OF GOD'S GREATNESS

At one point in Israel's history, God seeks to upgrade His people's holy fear by asking this question:

"To whom will you compare me? Who is my equal?" (Isaiah 40:25)

If there's ever been a time in history this question should be deeply pondered, and not just skimmed over, it's now. In this day and hour, mankind's "greatness" is continuously broadcasted on social media, mainstream media, television, and other platforms. The accolades of talented athletes, beautiful Hollywood stars, gifted musical artists, business gurus, charismatic leaders, and other important individuals are constantly showcased. Their fame is lauded, and though seemingly harmless, this constant feed of man's glory deters us from considering and pondering the reality of God's glory.[1]

Lisa and I ran headlong into this approximately twenty-five years ago in raising our four sons. In those days, the flow of information wasn't as prevalent because we didn't have apps and social media. Even then, we'd noticed our sons were a little too interested in a certain professional basketball player. At the time he was the most popular athlete in America and idolized by many, and even decades later his fame is intact.

Our family was ministering on the East Coast, and we were staying in a hotel on the ocean's shore. We'd just returned to our room after a few hours on the beach. The boys had been tossed and tumbled by a rough Atlantic Ocean and were both overjoyed and awed by its power.

I sat down for a talk with our three oldest sons. Pointing out the opened sliding glass doors, I questioned them. "Boys, that's a massive ocean out there, isn't it?"

In unison, they answered, "Yeah, Dad."

I continued, "You can only see a couple miles of it, but the ocean actually goes on for thousands of miles."

Wrapped in the warmth of their towels, the boys responded, "Wow!"

"And this one isn't even the biggest ocean; there is another, even bigger, called the Pacific Ocean. Then there are two more besides these two."

The boys all nodded in silent wonder as we continued to listen to the power of the pounding surf outside our opened door.

At the time of our trip, the NBA playoffs were in full swing. The achievements of that basketball superstar were continually being talked about by the press, ESPN, our sons, and their friends. My boys had been impressed by how easily he could palm (hold in one hand) a basketball. Knowing that to some degree my sons had grasped the overwhelming amount of water I'd just described, I asked, "Boys, do you know God weighed all the water you see, plus all that I have just described, in the palm of His hand?" (Isaiah 40:12). Their faces registered genuine amazement.

Then in the simplest terms possible I shared not just the size but the power of the ocean. I shared with our sons that if a meteor one mile wide were to hit the Atlantic Ocean a few hundred miles off the coast of New York City, it would create a wave large enough to wipe out every city's structure on the entire East Coast of America, the Caribbean, and much of South

America's Atlantic Coast![2] Not only that, but it would continue across the ocean and wreak havoc on several European and African coastal cities as well. Yet this wave would not be nearly as tall as the Atlantic is deep. So I asked, "What would happen if the entire weight of the ocean waters were unleashed against mankind? There is a lot of power in the oceans of the world, yet God weighed every drop of that water in the palm of His hand!"

I then turned to discuss the night sky. I asked the boys, who were now captivated, "Do you know what else the Bible says about how great God is?"

"What, Dad?"

"It says that God can measure the universe with the span of His hand" (Isaiah 40:12). Holding my hand before them, I demonstrated that a span is the distance from the tip of my thumb to the tip of my pinkie. What I asked our sons on that day is now what I'll ask you here: "Have you pondered the size of the universe?" It's beyond our mental capacities. Maybe if we attempt to catch a glimpse of the vastness of the universe, we'll come closer to getting a peek at His glory.

What I am about to write is a little technical, but I urge you to continue as I try to make it plain and simple, just as I did for our sons. When we think through these facts, it raises a sense of awe within us of His greatness, for we are told, "The heavens proclaim the glory of God" (Psalm 19:1).

Scientists estimate that there are billions of galaxies in the universe, with each of them containing approximately 100 million stars. The sizes of these galaxies are quite small compared to the space that exists between them.

Our sun is located in one of these galaxies. Our galaxy is so vast that when you look out into the sky at night you are not getting a picture of the universe, rather only the wee galaxy (compared to the universe) we live in, which is called the Milky Way. To take it a little further, you are not even getting a picture of the entire Milky Way but only a portion of it, for most of the stars in our galaxy are too far away to be seen by the naked eye.

So let's just talk about the stars we *can* see with our naked eye each night. The closest star to our earth other than our sun is a star that is only 4.3 light-years away. Now, to most this means very little, so let's expound. Light travels at the speed of 186,282 miles per second—not per hour but per *second*. That is roughly 670,000,000 miles per hour. Our airplanes fly approximately 500 miles per hour. So, as you can see, light is unimaginably fast!

To give you an idea of how fast this is, let's assume you could fly a jumbo jet to the sun. When I fly to Asia, which is on the other side of the earth from where I live, it takes me approximately twenty-three hours. If I took that same plane on a nonstop flight to our sun it would take roughly twenty-one years! Think about where you were twenty-one years ago, and then imagine spending all of the time from then until now sitting on an airplane (hopefully you have a window seat). For those who prefer driving . . . well, it couldn't be done, for it would take roughly two hundred years, not including any gas or rest stops! Now let's ask how long it takes for light to travel to the earth? The answer is a mere 8 minutes and 20 seconds!

Let's leave the sun and move on to the nearest star. We already know it is 4.3 light-years from the earth. If we built a scale model of the earth, sun, and nearest star, it would be as follows. In proportion, the earth would reduce to the size of a peppercorn, and the sun would become the size of an eight-inch-diameter ball. According to this scale, the distance from the earth to the sun would be twenty-six yards—a quarter of the length of a football field. Yet remember, for a scale airplane to span that twenty-six-yard distance, it would take more than twenty-one years.

So if this is the earth's and sun's models, can you guess how far the nearest star would be to our peppercorn earth? Would you think a thousand yards, two thousand, or maybe a mile? Not even close. Our nearest star would be placed four thousand miles away from the peppercorn! That means if you put our peppercorn earth in New York City, the sun, which takes twenty-one years to fly to, would be twenty-six yards away in New York City, and the nearest star on our scale model would be positioned past Los Angeles, 1,000 miles farther out in the Pacific Ocean! To reach this closest star by airplane would take approximately 51 *billion* years, nonstop! That's 51,000,000,000 years! Yet light from this star travels to earth in only 4.3 years!

Let's expand further. Most of the stars you see at night with the naked eye are one hundred to one thousand light-years away. However, there are a few stars you can see with the naked eye that are as far as four thousand light-years away (remember, those are not even the farthest stars in our tiny galaxy). I wouldn't even attempt to calculate the amount of time it would take for a plane to reach just one of these stars. But think of it: when you walk out at night and look at one of those stars that are 4,000 light-years away, you are actually looking at the light that left that star about the time Abraham married Sarah and has been traveling at a speed of 670,000,000 miles per hour without slowing down since and is just now getting to the earth!

Remember, these are just stars in our tiny galaxy called the Milky Way. We haven't even ventured out to the other billions of galaxies! And don't forget there is mostly vast space between the galaxies! For example, we have a very close neighboring galaxy that is named Andromeda. Its distance from us is approximately 2.3 million light-years away! Think of it—it takes light traveling at a speed of 670,000,000 miles per hour over two million years to get to our earth from that galaxy! And it is our closest neighboring galaxy. There are billions of others! Have we gone beyond our ability to compre-hend yet?

Let me remind you again, Isaiah declares that God measured this vast universe from His thumb to His pinky! In fact, Solomon declares by the Spirit of God, "But will God indeed dwell on the earth? Behold, heaven and the heaven of heavens cannot contain You" (1 Kings 8:27 NKJV). Are you getting a glimpse of who we are discussing?

After sharing all of this with our sons, the NBA superstar's status came back into a proper perspective. They were no longer in an unhealthy awe of his talents after pondering the greatness of our Creator.

But for you, the reader, I'd like to take this one step further. Not only has our Father in heaven done astonishing works of great size and proportion, but His details declare His glory as well. Science has spent years and enor-mous amounts of money to study the workings of this natural world. They still only have a small portion of the wisdom that went into His creation. There are still many unanswered questions. His designs and building blocks remain a marvel.

All forms of created life are based on cells. Cells are the building blocks of the human body, plants, animals, and every other living thing. The human body, which in itself is an engineering wonder, contains approximately 100,000,000,000,000 cells (Can you comprehend that number?!) of which there is a vast variety. In His wisdom, God designated these cells to perform specific tasks. They grow, multiply, and eventually die—right on schedule.

Though invisible to the naked eye, cells are not the smallest particles known to man. Cells consist of numerous tiny structures called molecules, and molecules are composed of even smaller structures called elements— and within elements can be found even tinier structures called atoms.

Atoms are so small that the period at the end of this sentence contains more than a billion of them. As minute as an atom is, it is made up almost entirely of empty space. The rest of the atom is composed of protons, neutrons, and electrons. Protons and neutrons are found clustered together in a minuscule and extremely dense nucleus at the very center of the atom. Little bundles of energy called electrons whiz around this nucleus at the speed of light. These are the core building blocks that hold all things together.

So where does the atom get its energy? And what force holds its energetic particles together? Scientists call it *electromagnetic and nuclear forces*. These are merely fancy scientific terms describing what still cannot be fully explained. For God has already said He is "upholding all things by the word of His power" (Hebrews 1:3 NKJV). And Colossians 1:17 says, "In him all things hold together" (NIV).

Stop and think this through. Here is this glorious Creator we call Father, whom even the universe cannot contain. He can measure the universe with the span of His hand, yet He is so detailed in His design of the tiny earth and the creatures who roam it that it leaves modern science with many unanswered questions after years of study. No wonder the psalmist cries out:

> I look at your heavens, which you made with your fingers. I see the moon and stars, which you created. But why are people even important to you? Why do you take care of human beings? (Psalm 8:3–4 NCV)

I think that sums it up. If I had to guess, the psalmist is probably uttering the thoughts of one of the massive angels who surround God's throne. They continue to cry "holy" due to the enormity and expanse of His awesomeness. These very beings watched Him create the vast universe and its complexity, then they saw the creation of humans and cried out, "What is this? Why does God give such attention to these little specks of people on this little speck of a planet?"

After my talk with my boys, they weren't swept into and consumed by the glory of our celebrities of modern times. They understood that anything great on our planet pales in comparison to the greatness of our God. I hope this appendix has done the same for you. Ponder what you've read in the light of the question God asked His people through the prophet Isaiah: "To whom will you compare Me? Who is My equal?" (Isaiah 40:25).

Of course, many books can be written on the wonders and wisdom of His creation. That is not my intent here. My purpose is to awaken amazement and wonder at the works of His hands, for they declare His great glory!

NOTES

Author Note

1. Take your small group or your whole church through *The Awe of God* video Bible study. With John Bevere as your guide, dig deeper into what God's Word says about the fear of the Lord and learn how to live out this healthy, holy virtue. Look for *The Awe of God Bible Study Guide + Streaming Video* at your favorite bookstore. Group pricing, sermon outlines, and church resources available at ChurchSource.com.

Introduction

1. Spurgeon, Charles. "Charles H. Spurgeon Quote," Quotefancy. Accessed November 15, 2022. https://quotefancy.com/quote/786372/Charles-H -Spurgeon-The-fear-of-God-is-the-death-of-every-other-fear-like-a-mighty -lion-it.

Chapter 1

1. Ecclesiastes 1:8 MSG
2. Ecclesiastes 1:9
3. Ecclesiastes 7:1
4. Ecclesiastes 1:15
5. Ecclesiastes 12:2–6

Chapter 3

1. The Complete Word Study Dictionary
2. Webster, Noah. "Awe." In *Webster's 1828 American Dictionary of the English Language*. Editorium, 2010.

Chapter 5

1. Hebrews 12:29 tells us God is a "consuming fire"; Romans 8:15 tells us He is Abba Father.

Chapter 6

1. *Butler's Lives of the Saints: Concise Edition Revised & Updated,* Michael Walsh, ed. (New York: HarperSanFrancisco, 1991), 29–30.

Chapter 8

1. "How Many Grains of Sand Are in One Square Inch?" WikiAnswers, accessed September 10, 2022, https://math.answers.com/other-math /How_many_grains_of_sand_are_in_one_square_inch.

Chapter 11

1. Johannes P. Louw and Eugene Albert Nida, *Greek-English Lexicon of the New Testament: Based on Semantic Domains* (New York: United Bible Societies, 1996), 684.
2. Louw and Nida, *Greek-English Lexicon of the New Testament: Based on Semantic Domains,* 540.
3. "Signs of Decline & Hope among Key Metrics of Faith: Barna Access." barna. gloo.us, 2021. https://barna.gloo.us/articles/signs-of-decline-and-hope.

Chapter 12

1. Louw and Nida, 765.

Chapter 13

1. See Luke 5:14; John 6:15; Philippians 2:7 NKJV; Hebrews 5:4; & Isaiah 42:2

Chapter 15

1. Spiros Zodhiates, *The Complete Word Study Dictionary: New Testament* (Chattanooga, TN: AMG Publishers, 2000).
2. Louw and Nida, 433.

Chapter 16

1. Louw and Nida, 429.
2. Leon Morris, *The Gospel according to Matthew,* The Pillar New Testament Commentary (Grand Rapids, MI; Leicester, England: W.B. Eerdmans; Inter-Varsity Press, 1992), 175.

Chapter 19

1. C. S. Lewis and Clyde S. Kilby, *C.S. Lewis: Letters to an American Lady* (Grand Rapids, MI: Eerdmans, 1997).

Chapter 20

1. Louw and Nida, 662.

Chapter 29

1. "Intimate Definition and Meaning: Collins English Dictionary," Intimate definition and meaning | Collins English Dictionary (HarperCollins Publishers Ltd), accessed November 15, 2022, https://www.collinsdictionary .com/us/dictionary/english/intimate; "*intimus*"–WordSense Online Dictionary (15th November 2022) URL: https://www.wordsense.eu/intimus/

Chapter 35

1. Louw and Nida, 375.
2. See John 3:1–2; 6:26, 66; 12:42; 19:38; Matthew 26:14–16.

Chapter 38

1. Merriam-Webster.com Dictionary, s.v. "legacy," accessed November 1, 2022, https://www.merriam-webster.com/dictionary/legacy.
2. Ludwig Koehler et al., *The Hebrew and Aramaic Lexicon of the Old Testament* (Leiden: E. J. Brill, 1994–2000), 217.
3. Warren Baker and Eugene E. Carpenter, *The Complete Word Study Dictionary: Old Testament* (Chattanooga, TN: AMG Publishers, 2003), 231.
4. Richard Louis Dugdale, *The Jukes: A Study of Crime, Pauperism, Disease and Heredity*, Georgia State University College of Law Reading Room, January 1, 1969, https://readingroom.law.gsu.edu/cgi/viewcontent. cgi?article=1000&context=buckvbell.
5. Robert Alan Ward, "The Descendants of Jonathan Edwards," White Mountain Independent, September 27, 2019, https://www.wmicentral .com/community_beat/religion/the-descendants-of-jonathan-edwards /article_9e54e16d-59c5–5cf2-a99f-dea187da978a.html.

Chapter 39

1. The proper understanding of this Hebrew word is the lure or bait placed in a hunter's trap.Warren Baker and Eugene E. Carpenter, *The Complete Word*

Study Dictionary: Old Testament (Chattanooga, TN: AMG Publishers, 2003), 585.

2. Baker and Carpenter, *The Complete Word Study Dictionary: Old Testament*, 18.

Chapter 42

1. Jon Turteltaub, dir., *National Treasure*, (2005; Burbank, CA: Walt Disney Entertainment), 2005, DVD.

Appendix B

1. Facts and figures are from a book I wrote years ago, *A Heart Ablaze,* in Chapter 4, titled "The Glory of the Lord" (Nashville, TN: Thomas Nelson, 1999), 31–44.

2. Since I first wrote this, better scientific models have been created. According to research, coastal towns may be okay if a meteor hits the middle of the ocean. But no one knows for sure what would happen. Here are some interesting articles on the speculation: https://www.nytimes.com/1998/01/08/us/what-if-huge-asteroid-hits-atlantic-you-don-t-want-to-know.html and https://www.space.com/35081-asteroid-impact-ocean-computer-simulations-solar-system.html.

ABOUT THE AUTHOR

John Bevere is a minister known for his bold, uncompromising approach to God's Word. He is also an international bestselling author who has written more than 20 books that have, collectively, sold millions of copies and been translated into 129 languages. Along with his wife, Lisa, John is the co-founder of Messenger International—a ministry committed to revolutionizing global discipleship. Driven by a passion to develop uncompromising followers of Christ, Messenger has given over 56 million translated resources to leaders across the globe. To extend these efforts, the MessengerX app was developed, providing translated, digital discipleship resources at no cost to users in 121 languages and counting. MessengerX currently has users in over 20,000 cities and 230 nations. When John is home in Franklin, Tennessee, you'll find him loving on his g-babies, playing pickleball, or trying to convince Lisa to take up golf.

Loved reading The Awe of God?
Give it away!

If reading this book impacted you and you'd like more copies for those in your sphere of influence (perhaps your church, small group, company, friends, or family), please reach out to my team at mail@messengerinternational.org or 1-800-648-1477 to get a discount on a bulk order!

Free Courses, Audiobooks & More to Help You Grow in Your Faith.

The MessengerX app is a revolutionary tool that connects you with world-class teachers, authors, and leaders who will help you embrace a vibrant faith in your everyday life.

Scan the QR code to dowload MessengerX

MessengerX

Drawing Near

John Bevere

God desires a close relationship with us! But far too many settle for a shallow one when God has extended an invitation to draw near, so we can all experience greater depths of intimacy with Him. Learn how you can transform a boring and lifeless relationship with God into one that is energizing and exhilarating!

Watch

BOOKS BY JOHN

Messenger International was founded by John and Lisa Bevere in 1990. Since its inception, Messenger International's God-entrusted messages have transformed millions of lives worldwide. Our mission is to develop uncompromising followers of Christ who transform our world.

Call: 1-800-648-1477

Email: Mail@MessengerInternational.org

Visit us online at: MessengerInternational.org

Connect with John Bevere:

JohnBevere.com